A Peaceful Start

365 Daily Messages of Hope, Inspiration, and Insight for Inner Peace

BY

Luann Smith

A Peaceful Start: 365 Daily Messages of Hope, Inspiration, and Insight for Inner Peace

Published by

Woodpecker Press, LLC

www.WoodpeckerPress.com

ISBN: 978-1-937397-50-0 (sc)

ISBN: 978-1-937397-51-7 (epub)

Cover Design: Nu-Image Design

Dedication

To my friend and late mentor Toot,
Thank you for loving me until I could love myself.

Acknowledgments

I would like to express my gratitude to everyone involved in making this book happen:

- To Almighty God, without whom I am an illusion
- To all my friends at Second Street who continue to raise the dead
- To Lisa Romeo, my editor, for helping me bring my manuscript to life
- To Donna Thompson, my publisher, for all her support and continued guidance in making my book a reality

Table of Contents

Introduction

Waking up ready to begin the day with a positive attitude is the peaceful path. Yet too often we awaken with a head full of negativity—an awful way to start the day. When this is a daily occurrence, it's no wonder you're stressed out and your life isn't changing. Beginning today, with *A Peaceful Start*, you can change that and get your day off to a positive start. Simply take a moment each morning with your coffee or tea and read a page and think about the message. (I even dated them for you, though you can start any day of the year). With each day's encouragement, you can get your thinking going in the right direction, resulting in a more peaceful way to go about your day. Little by little, day by day, by reading—and acting upon—these daily messages, you will begin to see positive changes in your life and go from blaming to blessing.

You see, it's the thoughts we harbor that are the culprit. Our thoughts and attitude—not how your co-worker spoke to you today or what your partner is or isn't doing for you—are what sabotage us. It's how you think about and then react to what happens that determines your chances of living a happy and fulfilled life on a daily basis. You do have choices, beginning with changing your thinking. Right thinking leads to right actions and positive thoughts lead to a positive life.

Anyone can do this if they have the desire to change. No matter what your circumstances, gender, sexual preference, religion, or age, this book will meet you wherever you are in your thinking and awaken you to the power of positive thinking. That power lives within us all.

I follow spiritual principles and will talk about God as this is my personal belief. But I also believe there are many roads that lead to faith, which also work; I have an open mind, and I respect them all. I have tried to write with honesty and sincerity, sharing my own personal experiences. Some topics will be covered more than once. I feel they have significant value in our lives and are beneficial to finding peace, so I addressed them more frequently. I believe there is something for everyone in the following pages, everyone who seeks a more peaceful way to live.

My life is a testament to the power of positive thinking. I was once at death's door, circling the drain, addicted to drugs and alcohol. Blaming others, the circumstances in my life, and even God for everything that was happening to me. But after simultaneously having a nervous breakdown and then a spiritual awakening, I came to see that it was solely my own way of thinking that had gotten me to the negative place. Not anything or anyone else.

I then looked into that mirror I had avoided my whole life and finally saw what the problem was—she was staring back at me. That was the bottom I needed to hit in order to change and, with the help of God and others, I turned my life around. One key method I adopted was keeping positive thoughts as the focus of each day, while staying grounded in my faith. Practicing morning prayer and meditation helps me generate the peaceful thoughts and behavior that help control my reactions to the events that challenge me throughout the day and threaten my peace.

My hope is that by reading a new page in this book each morning, you can approach your day with enthusiasm, a grateful heart, and a positive attitude, leading to a more peaceful life.

Luann Smith

January 1

HAPPY NEW YOU!

Don't put it off any longer. Whatever it is, do it now! You know, that change you've been wanting to make that has been whirling around in your mind and never leaves? It's been calling to you. Let today be the day you answer. Every new beginning starts with the first step. So, go for it! A new year is beginning. Why not start with a new you today? Your best version of yourself is waiting for you. Start by taking a few steps…or a lot of steps. Begin making the necessary changes that will bring you to your goals. Outline your plan of action and create a new reality for yourself by making the decision to do something different and sticking to it, remembering that consistency and diligence are the bookends we need to succeed and become new. Go forth with your faith and Happy New You!

January 2

COINCIDENCES?

You have been thinking of a friend you haven't seen in a while and they suddenly send you a text or appear at the grocery store. While at work, you meet the new hire and they have exactly the information you needed for a project. Ever wonder why these things happen? Some call them coincidences, but I have come to believe these seemingly trivial chance encounters are not coincidences at all. These happenstances were meant to be. God puts people in our lives exactly when we need them. They show up just in time with the guidance we need at that moment, which can be life-changing. Words you needed to hear enlighten your mind and everything suddenly makes sense. You have been awakened and emerge with a new awareness of yourself. Or conversely, we sometimes have a message for them. Either way, be open when these chance encounters happen; something very special often occurs.

January 3

FAKE IT 'TIL YOU MAKE IT

Some days when I awake, I am immobilized by indifference—overwhelmed with my life and feeling anxious. I want to pull the covers over my head and hide. At those times, moving out of bed is like pushing a truck uphill by myself. But I have found that taking action is the only remedy against this negativity. Those are the days when I go into my "Fake it 'til you make it" mode. I push myself and put one foot in front of the other, carrying on as if all is well. Meanwhile, I pray for strength, continue moving my feet, doing what needs to be done, and mentally start making a gratitude list for the day. This is so necessary to break down the walls of indifference within me. Saying out loud how grateful I am—for my health, my family, my job, my dog, or whatever is important in my life—melts away the ice around my frozen heart and eventually, the words I speak have meaning and feeling behind them. The journey from my head to my heart is complete and I rise above the anxiety and fear. Now, I'm no longing faking it, but making it.

January 4

ATTITUDE OF GRATITUDE

Find something to be grateful for today and bathe in it all day.
With just a little thought, you'll realize there are so many things you
could put on that gratitude list. Start with what we take for granted
every day—simple things like our sight, our hands, or our feet.
Once you get started, more will come to you and your list will grow.
Gratitude is contagious! It builds upon itself and before you know it,
concentrating on gratitude will bring a sense of peace that will wash
over you. Life is full of wonderful things to be happy about once
you open your heart and mind. When you arrive at this attitude of
gratitude, spread some cheer to all you meet. Co-workers, people on
the checkout line at the store, or anyone anywhere. Be a beacon of
gratitude to all you meet today.

January 5

ENTITLEMENT

In our household as children, we had to earn everything; rewards were only for good behavior. This taught us true appreciation for all that we had, and I will always be grateful to my parents for teaching us this valuable lesson, which took work and effort on their part. Their guidance and consistent example of rewarding us when we did a good job fostered the idea that working hard will always deliver great rewards. In contrast, giving kids too much without their earning it creates an attitude of entitlement; without some measure of discipline in giving, one can never learn true appreciation. We all want to give our children everything we never had but at what cost? Without boundaries, you risk robbing a child of learning to appreciate and value what they have; whereas, giving as a reward for good behavior will promote an attitude of true appreciation and only good can come from that. I have taken this lesson into my adult life, appreciating everything I have today, from material gains to valuable friendships with others.

January 6

LIVING IN THE NOW

Try to be fully present in each moment. How? Be where your feet are. If you find yourself mentally wandering, bring yourself back. Focus on what you are doing this very second, not what happened ten minutes ago or what may happen an hour from now. God is sending messages every day in each moment. We cannot hear the message if our focus is on yesterday or tomorrow. Linking our hearts and minds and living in the now will help us hear the message. Slow down your mind and listen to the still, small voice within you. It is there where we are led to our highest good. Our future is made up of all the decisions we make in the now; so rewrite yours by staying focused in the moment. By surrendering each moment to what is, therein lies our peace.

January 7

"JUST WAIT"

Sometimes when we hear those dreadful words, "Just wait," it can send us over the deep end. As we all know, waiting can be difficult. Waiting for the right opportunity to arrive, waiting for that special person to appear, waiting for the perfect job, or for the doctor to call with test results. Waiting can be nerve wracking, and practicing patience at these times is the last thing we want to do. We want answers NOW in our fast-paced lives. But, in reality, patience is the only thing that can get us through. Chasing and obsessing after outcomes will only prolong the anxiety and can be excruciating. Instead, we can try another approach. Quiet your mind and become still by using your favorite prayer. Saying it over and over, will have a calming effect by changing the flow of your thoughts, breaking the mental logjam, easing your mind back to peace. I have used this method in all of the above scenarios and it works. So now, hearing "just wait" does not have to be a death sentence.

January 8

YOUR BEST THINKING

There can be times when your best thinking becomes your worst nightmare. I've learned the hard way that even my best thinking could use a second opinion. Checking with others before acting on plans I've concocted is always best. Going it alone can be dangerous since we can all rationalize our behaviors to get what we want. In the past, I've made some decisions without consulting others, which made my life very difficult. Now, I take a different approach, which guarantees better judgment. Whenever I have an idea about changing something major in my life, or I have to make an important decision, before taking any action, I consult with trusted friends whose advice I respect. They will always have my best interest at heart and know me sometimes better than I know myself. This act also allows for God's will to enter into the equation. Seeking God is that simple. When I am willing to let go of outcomes, run things by others, and be open to listen, I can be confident in my decision making.

January 9

GOD IS MY SOURCE

When I find myself depending on a relationship, a job, or anything else for security, or feeling as though I cannot live without something or someone, I have made that person or situation more important than God. And that has always failed me! Depending on anything other than God will shut you off from the very source of help and guidance you need to survive and thrive. It's important to remember that everything in this world may be fleeting and can change in a New York minute. Jobs can be lost, relationships can end abruptly, your home can be destroyed by a hurricane. There is only one constant in the universe—God. So keep God first in all your affairs, and if a relationship fails, your job dissolves, or you lose your home in a hurricane, God will provide another channel through which good things will come. Remembering that God is my source will get me through anything I am facing.

January 10

YOU DID GOOD

Hearing "You did good" after performing tasks that are important to us always boosts our confidence. Whether it's in response to a work project, an athletic achievement, helping someone who needs a hand, building a house, or caring for the elderly, it gives me such a feeling of satisfaction hearing this from my work peers, friends, or family. Who doesn't feel wonderful when others acknowledge their work? These three simple words light a spark in me to want to do more. We all feel appreciated when our deeds are acknowledged. Saying this when others need to hear it is just as important and helps to promote their positive sense of self. We all need a pat on the back sometimes and being conscious of this can make a world of difference in other people's lives. This uplifting sentence should be used more often in every area of our lives from teachers, bosses, parents, partners, everyone, to create fulfillment and good will. After all, there is always something good we can find in any situation if we look closely enough, no matter what. So, don't hold back today. Tell someone who needs to hear it that they did well.

January 11

PICK UP AN OAR

One popular modern definition of insanity is "doing the same thing over and over and expecting different results." If you recognize yourself in that, aren't you tired of getting nowhere? Perhaps you are in bondage to an affliction that is ruling your life—drugs, alcohol, a failed relationship, dependency on people, or smoking. Whatever your affliction, now is the time to stop that repetitive behavior and break free. If you are ready to start over and become new, you can do it right now. Make the decision. You have the power within you to choose and when you make a new choice, you empower yourself. God put the power of free will in you when you were created. Tap into that free will to get a different result; don't do the same thing again. Changing ingrained habits is challenging and you often can't do it alone. I couldn't do it alone. I found a group of others in the same boat, and I had to pick up an oar and start rowing. There is strength in numbers. The longer you wait and rationalize your behavior, the longer it takes to get free. Make the decision now. Take action by taking that first step. Your freedom awaits you.

January 12

MIRACLES

I love miracles. I even love the sound of this precious word when it rolls off my lips. Miracles are happening every day to all kinds of people who have a sincere desire to change. Miracles show up when we humble ourselves to God by asking through prayer to change our thinking and help us walk in a different direction. We create a space for miracles to arrive by keeping the faith no matter how bleak the outlook. By changing our minds, and keeping focused on a new course, miracles are released in our lives and our perspective changes. We are reborn to a new way of life we never knew existed or one we thought we could ever embrace. How? That's the power of miracles.

January 13

GETTING NAKED IN TIMES SQUARE

I have lived so many lies in my life until I just couldn't do it
anymore. I had become a storyteller, fictionalizing everything,
and was completely lost within myself. One lie led to another and
covering up the lies became a full-time job. Each day, the anxiety
escalated as I created more turmoil in my life with this terrible
character flaw. My life was spinning out of control and it was time to
face the truth. I had to take off all the masks I was wearing and face
who I was once and for all. This painful process, which I think of as
the equivalent of getting naked in Times Square, was the only way to
find my true self. Through all the pain, I found there is true freedom
in honesty. Living my life without hiding anything is liberating.
Today, being "naked" isn't frightening because I'm honest about who
I am, no pretense, what you see is what you get. As a bonus, I now
attract honesty from others because I live in truth.

January 14

GOD IS THE SOLUTION

What's the question? God is the solution. Tell it to yourself today with whatever challenge you are facing. You have nothing to lose and everything to gain. Is it a new job you desire? God is the solution. Say it. Are you facing a health issue? God is the solution. Say it. If you lost your home in a hurricane, say it. If you're not sure how you will pay the bills this month, say it. Tell yourself, *God is the solution.* Why try to solve things on your own if you have a source of intelligence and power that is omniscient and always ready to help? By saying these words, you are turning things over to this power greater than yourself by asking for help. God *will* unleash the power and guidance you need. People will show up unexpectedly, jobs will appear, and even your health will improve by letting go of all the stresses. Seek God as the solution and be led to a better existence as everything falls into place in your life.

January 15

RUDE AWAKENING TO SPIRITUAL AWAKENING

For many years, I didn't want to feel, so I escaped pain by self-medicating. I continued this until I became addicted. If any problem arose, I got wasted and checked out. As my disease progressed, my problems mounted until I found myself facing certain death if I continued on that path of destruction. Thankfully, I had a moment of clarity which pierced through the denial I lived in for so long, and I realized how dire my situation was. I was sick and tired of being sick and tired. This was the day that would change my life. I finally hit that proverbial rock bottom and was able to surrender. I had a rude awakening followed by a spiritual awakening. My spirit was awakened, and I found God within me as the source of all good, as if a trap door opened up within me and the power I needed emerged. God's power has lifted me out of my addiction and keeps me sober each day as I continue to develop my personal relationship through prayer and meditation and grow my faith. I came to see this power resides in us all, ready to help us when we surrender and seek help.

January 16

BLESS EVERYTHING

Today, use your mind constructively rather than destructively. Build everything up rather than tearing it down. Try blessing everything and everyone you come into contact with today—and watch your life change. Our minds are receptacles for our thoughts, and our actions are just the outcome of those thoughts. In that way, we resemble computers and when a computer doesn't do what we need it to, there's usually one explanation: garbage in, garbage out. When I began using my mind for more positive ways of thinking, that's when abundance, happiness, peace, and love began to show up. This is the key to creating a happier and more harmonious life. We begin to attract what we think. Bless others and watch your blessings arrive.

January 17

MAKE TIME FOR GOD

My day begins with a daily visit with God through prayer and meditation. In the early morning, I am most open and my mind is not yet cluttered with the day's events—or, sometimes it is. Either way, taking time to pray and meditate makes my day run more smoothly. As I move through the world, I find I am better equipped to make good decisions because of that early morning practice. I come from a more peaceful place, not hurried and scattered or afraid. Why not begin your day by consulting with your Creator? God knows all about you and knows what's best for you. Becoming still and listening for direction makes all the difference in how your day will unfold. God is always ready when you are. Make time for God and you will receive the clarity you need for a more peaceful day.

January 18

DON'T WATER THE PLANT

If you don't water your plants, they will certainly die and wither away. The same is true of the negative thoughts we allow to fester in our minds: if we don't feed them, in time they will fade away. When I entertain negative thoughts about anyone or anything, allowing them to grow in my mind means they will flourish and I end up with resentments toward others. Eventually, the more negativity that takes root in my mind, the more miserable I become and I begin to attract other negative people since misery does love company. There is a simple solution: stop "watering" the plants of negative thinking that are undermining your peace and serenity, and let them die off.

January 19

MILK THE COW

Some days I take two steps forward and five steps back. While driving to work, I perform a random act of kindness, allowing two cars to merge in front of me, then a few blocks later, I flip the bird to someone for cutting me off. Such scrambled behavior drains the peace and goodness I work so hard to attain and which I'd promised myself to maintain in the course of the day. It's like milking the cow, pulling on those udders properly and steadily, working hard to fill up the can with wholesome milk, and then kicking over the can. Can you ever imagine a farmer doing this? Cancelling good deeds with one rage-filled action spills all my hard work to the ground. Today, make your positive actions count. Milk that cow and then protect that sweet, wholesome milk.

January 20

ROADBLOCKS OR SIGNPOSTS?

When my prayers are not answered because I didn't get what I wanted, I know from past experience it's because God has something better planned for me. My choice was not the right choice. I used to think of these occurrences as roadblocks but now see them as signposts to better things ahead. Now when I pray for something, I surrender it to God and ask for what I need and what's best for me. I put it in God's hands and trust in God's will for me. This thinking opens me up to opportunities I could have never imagined with my limited thinking. When I didn't get a raise and promotion I wanted and believed I deserved, it led me to pursue other work options, which I would have never otherwise done. Now I have a new career that is more fulfilling, and I am the happiest I have ever been at work. So, never worry when there are roadblocks; see them as signposts pointing you in a better direction on the spiritual highway.

January 21

PUT DOWN THAT UMBRELLA

Why sit around worrying about what you can't change or control? Worry is a big waste of energy and gets you nowhere, like carrying around an umbrella in the sunshine waiting for rain. Imagine how silly that is? Well, that's exactly what we do when we worry. We never know the outcomes of the events in our lives until they happen so why not enjoy the moment instead of stressing? What will be is going to be whether you spend your energy in a negative or positive way. So, release your worries, put down that umbrella, and enjoy what life is offering you at this very moment. Be at peace with yourself while you let God handle things. Start right now by moving your thoughts in a different direction and use your energy to create peace, living in anticipation of all God's goodness.

January 22

DIFFERENT IS DIFFERENT

Thoughtful planning is wise, but if all you do is sit around thinking about something and never get into action, you're stuck. Get yourself moving and do something—something different! We can always come up with a million excuses for not acting, sitting around doing nothing and then wonder, "Why is my life not changing?" If you want change and different results, you must put forth different actions. Different is different. Say it aloud to yourself so it sinks in. *Different is different.* Get it yet? Now, stop procrastinating and take different steps to make new things happen. The universe will only support change if you take different actions. One step will lead to the next and before you realize it, a new beginning emerges. You are reborn and are reaping the benefits of different actions instead of same old, same old.

January 23

TELL SOMEONE

Don't hold it in. Let it out. Sharing with others is healthy and will make a big difference, so tell someone how you're feeling. Keeping secrets leads to sickness on many levels. I suffer mentally, emotionally, and spiritually when I hide the regretful things that I have done or have been done to me. Feelings of embarrassment, guilt, remorse, and resentment fill my body, mind, and soul with poison as I continually beat myself up, compounding the pain and guilt. When this happens, I have found that cleansing myself is necessary to restore my well-being. When I tell someone, my problems are cut in half and I don't have to go it alone anymore. I can call a trusted friend, unburden myself, and escape my self-constructed prison by honestly and openly sharing my secrets. This allows me to forgive myself, forgive others, and begin healing, empowering me on the road to freedom, all because I told someone.

January 24

THEY DON'T FEEL A THING

I used to spend a lot of time tearing down others, loving a good gossip session with friends, until I found how much it hurts me. You may think, on the surface, gossip seems harmless since the other person does not hear what you say about them. But, this kind of behavior is detrimental to us too, if we look at it honestly. Hurtful words about others always hurt the speaker more than the recipients. They don't feel a thing. Gossiping diminishes any peace we strive for and separates us from the good within us. I have found that building myself up at the expense of others is an ego-feeding proposition that will ultimately undermine my peace and serenity by giving me a false sense of being superior. When I indulge in gossip, I pay a big price. It separates me from our shared humanity, when we are all equal as children of a loving God. Now, when I find myself indulging in gossip, I stop, remember this is mean-spirited, and quickly begin to point out the nice things about that other person, turning it around.

January 25

SACRIFICE

In our day-to-day lives we sometimes find ourselves running around thinking about our next challenge of the day, focusing only on ourselves. We get so caught up in our own stuff we begin to stress. My remedy, when I find myself in this spot, is to get out of myself by performing a sacrifice and helping another. I take a step back, disengage from what I'm doing, and think of something I can do for another to make their day better. It doesn't have to be a grand gesture, it's simply putting someone or something before myself and whatever I am doing. This frees me from worry and stress. Sacrifice is a very spiritual act that benefits the giver as well as the receiver. Both emerge equally blessed and peace returns. Try it. Give of yourself to another and watch where that one small sacrifice leads you.

January 26

WHERE IS GOD IN ALL THIS?

Where is God in all this? Now either God is or isn't. What's it going to be? Good question. I usually ask myself this question when I run out of options and have no more answers for how to fix things in my life. I then realize I have been running my life on self-will, forgetting who I am and have made myself God. This is where the rubber meets the road for me. By suffering through the anxiety, I'm humbled into submission and begin inviting my Creator back into my life, realigning my will with the goodness within me. I think of all the miracles God has bestowed upon my life and then remind myself of a simple truth. Either God is or I'm an illusion. My life is a testament of the power of God working through me and no matter what worldly illusions I fall asleep to, I will never be the same again. I have been blessed beyond what the human eyes can see and brought up and out of hell, delivered from death's door. The power of God's love has touched my life and I will never be the same again. When I forget and get caught up in the trivial, mundane things of this world, I am always led back to, "Where is God in all this?" Asking this is my saving grace.

January 27

LOOK BUT DON'T STARE

Mistakes from our past can be overwhelming when we think of them. Looking back at the wreckage of my past used to make me very uncomfortable and filled me with fear and regrets. But confronting the past was necessary and continues to be a very important part of my healing and growing. I had to look back with honesty in order to move forward. Doing so helped me gain vital knowledge about my negative behaviors and acknowledge my own part in the situation. Learning from the past is a very rewarding experience when you uncover patterns that caused harm to yourself and others and then use that knowledge as a catalyst for change. However, I've found it's best to *look but don't stare* at your past. Staring can cause us to get stuck, and this will bring more guilt and remorse. Glance, extract what you need, and move on. Look but don't stare.

January 28

BURNING HOUSE

So many times when I was upset, I would try to figure out and analyze my behaviors and where I went wrong. Focusing on my mistakes while I am still experiencing the aftermath just upsets me more. When I'm still stuck in the mistake, I never get answers, just more problems added to my woes. Trying to analyze my thinking when I'm upset is like walking through a house that is on fire and trying to figure out how the fire started. Would I ever do that? Never! If a house is on fire, I would run out immediately! Now when I'm upset, I get myself centered once again and concentrate on putting the fire out first. Once that's accomplished, I know that later on, I will have a better perspective to look back and see what I can learn. I will find my answers then, much like the fire inspector who waits until the fire's out before looking through the ashes for the cause.

January 29

CHANGE, THE INSIDE JOB

I needed to change. I thought if I cut my hair, hung around different people, or changed my job, a new person would emerge. But changing the exterior never worked. It just changed the exterior. Finally, after going through a lot of pain, I was motivated to look within and there is where I found I have the power to truly change. Change begins as an inside job. If I'm looking for something outside of myself to change me, I am off and will continue to be stuck. No new look, person, job, institution, or relationship has that power. Only the power of God working through me does. By aligning myself with this power, by daily visits through meditation and prayer, I strengthen my relationship with my Creator and receive the necessary power needed to enact the change, from inside. So be it.

January 30

BREAKDOWN, THEN BREAKTHROUGH

Don't be afraid of having a breakdown. For some of us, that's what it takes to find our peace. That's what it took for me. My breakdown led me to a breakthrough, a rite of passage to a spiritual awakening and finding a God of my own understanding. Spiritual awakenings can come through pain or from voluntarily reaching for them. Mine, of course, came through much pain. But don't be afraid of the breakdown, of pain, or of feeling your emotions. Feel the feelings, then let them go. Let them pass through you, for God is on the other side waiting to catch you and introduce you to who and what you really are. We feel emotions but we are not our emotions; we are so much more. A breakdown can be a healing experience, which will show you how strong you really are; you will never be the same again. You will become comfortable in your own skin and a new person will emerge from the ashes. The peace and serenity I desperately searched for my whole life came after having a breakdown. This is what it often takes to find your true self. Your breakthrough awaits.

January 31

COURAGE DOES NOT COME IN A BOTTLE

Courage was something I kept in a bottle of vodka or in a vial of cocaine. I always had it with me and when needed, I used to drink my courage or snort it up my nose. Need to speak up for myself, boom—take out the vial and snort some courage. Need to tell someone how I really feel, boom—take out the vodka and swig some courage. While under the influence, I could do or say anything to anyone. But today, I know better and I no longer seek courage in a vial or a bottle because I know it's already within me. I don't need to take a substance outside myself, because true courage arrives when we leave those substitutes behind and walk through fear with God. These things are not easy to do but are necessary to get to the other side of fear and find our authentic courage. Much like working out at the gym, when we work our courage muscle, it gets stronger. Now, I feel the fear but walk in faith knowing that doing the right thing will become easier as my courage increases each time I face life without the consequences of being under the influence of a drug. Oh, how sweet that kind of courage is!

February 1

WORTHLESS TO WORTHY

How do you respond when you receive an unexpected gift or compliment from a friend? Do you say, "No, you shouldn't have," or do you receive it with thanksgiving? Your response will show you a lot about how you really feel about yourself. I remember once, a friend gave me a book he thought would be interesting and helpful to me. I wasn't expecting it and it was a very nice gesture of kindness on his part. However, when he handed me the book, my response was awful. I went into a diatribe of excuses as to why he shouldn't have given me the book and how foolish he was to do such a thing! Clearly, that was the wrong response. A simple "thank you" would have sufficed. I had to take a look at myself and find out why I was acting this way. Through honesty and self-reflection, I saw how this reaction was embedded in my psyche for most of my life and had become an automatic response over the years. Upon further examination, I came to see I had little self-worth and didn't feel I deserved kindness from others. This deep insecurity within me stemmed from a lack of worthiness I had my whole life about myself, and I needed to change if I was to ever find peace. The good news is that by uncovering these insecurities, you can change through the process of self-honesty, self-examination, and taking different actions. I started to say "thank you" to anyone who did anything remotely nice for me, and over time I went from feeling worthless to worthy. By feeding myself positive messages, I started to believe I deserved all the good that came into my life and today know that I am worthy.

February 2

TIME TO CHANGE THE CHANNEL

Seeing the good in others is my goal each day, but some days are a
challenge. I fall short and end up taking other people's inventory
instead of my own. When I find myself being critical and judgmental
of others, it's time to change the channel. My mind is similar to a
TV with my thoughts as the channels and I can change them at any
time. I am just a thought away from seeing others through the eyes
of love instead of fear. We all have our weaknesses and it's up to each
of us to work on ourselves, accept one another, and not critique each
other. God gives me the choice each moment to decide how I want
to see others and when I make the wrong choice, I can always correct
it by changing the channel. Instead of focusing on the things I think
are wrong in others, instead I pick something positive about them
and build on that.

February 3

TRY GOOD REPETITION

Doing things in a negative manner again and again is using bad repetition. Doing things over and over in a positive manner is using good repetition. One thing is for sure: if we do something continually, we are going to get results, either good or bad. Each day we get to choose how to expend our energy and choose who we want to be. So why not use that energy for good and try good repetition? Repeat good behaviors until they become a part of you and let negative behaviors fall away like rotten fruit that falls from a tree. I continually smoked cigarettes and was slowly suffocating myself. Then one day, thankfully, I wanted to quit. I used good repetition and formed new habits to help heal me, and I was blessed to be able to finally quit smoking! When you use good repetition, it heals you and gives your life a new perspective. A new person emerges from within, changing you at your core. Put all your energy into forming new healing habits of good repetition.

February 4

COMPLACENCY

Are you growing and moving forward in your life or are you backsliding? We are never standing still, since standing still is an illusion. I know for myself that if I'm not moving forward, I'm backsliding and become complacent. Complacency is that stagnant place we end up in when we don't have a clear purpose of what we should be doing each day in our lives. When I wake up and throw the day to the winds and have no plan of action for myself, I end up never getting anywhere except on the couch. We justify and feed ourselves excuses for not having a plan for the day, such as we can get to it later or we need a break. However, either way you want to cut the cookie, this is what complacency looks like. Fear is always at the root of complacency, and fear will render you immobile if you don't work against it. So, don't fall for the lie you are telling yourself or you will become bored and boredom will lead to trouble. Give yourself a reason to get out of bed each day and wake up with a plan to continue your life in a forward, positive motion. Have great expectations and a clear vision of who and what you want to become, stepping into the part. We are at our best when we dedicate our lives to becoming the best version of ourselves that we can be, and this will have a rippling effect for those around us on how to succeed by not falling into complacency.

February 5

CELEBRATE OUR DIFFERENCES

Our world is like a rainbow with all different types of people and personalities joining together producing a beautiful, colorful place. When hearts are joined, that rainbow is in perfect harmony. Imagine how boring it would be if we were all the same. God created us all different for a reason. We all have a lot to learn from one another. Our differences make us unique. Don't let differences hold you back from enjoying a new friendship with a co-worker, someone you meet at a party, or at the grocery store just because they are different. When we celebrate differences, the whole world opens up for us; our lives are enriched with love that goes beyond appearances to the deeper connection we all share as children of a loving God.

February 6

MAKE THOSE ALTERATIONS

If we can alter clothing to fit our body, why can't we alter our life to find a better fit too? The good news is, we can. With God's help, I have altered my life and created a more peaceful space for myself—removing toxic people, places, and behavior along the way. Letting go of relationships that have caused me harm and prevented me from peace is the biggest alteration I have had to make. I realized I didn't need to keep toxic people in my life, and neither do you. Removing them may be painful and awkward at first, but eventually you'll find your life feels more comfortable because of the alteration. Staying stuck in relationships that don't serve your highest good wastes precious time you could be spending with those you truly love and who will nurture you. Make your alterations now and start your new way of loving yourself.

February 7

THAT LAST WORD

Walking away from an argument is difficult, especially if you're certain you are right. Getting in that last word was what I lived for because it gave me such a feeling of power. Those "drop the mic" moments when I verbally triumphed put me in a state of euphoria, and I loved the high. But following every high comes the low, and there is a price we pay for angry outbursts. When I began losing relationships and jobs, it was time to change. I had to learn a new way to handle myself when an argument erupted, so I started practicing self-restraint by walking away. I literally removed myself from the ruckus. This helped me disengage from the anger and quiet the disturbance within me. Over time and through daily practice, the power of choice returned and I can now *choose* to be happy or *choose* to be angry. Having the last word and winning useless arguments serves no purpose but to feed anger, escalate the argument, and keep you in the loop of craziness. When I walk away now, the last word for me is peace.

February 8

ALONE TIME

Spend some time enjoying the quiet. Take a long walk on the beach with no one but your thoughts and God. How about sitting alone on your deck meditating about God and nature? These are some of the ways I spend time alone with God. Solitude, or "alone time" as I call it, feeds your soul and nurtures your spirit. It helps me to remain peaceful and sane in our fast-paced world, and so I make it a daily ritual. Once I made it a part of my daily routine, alone time changed my life, a time out to reconnect with my spirit and replenish my peace and well-being. I put myself into a peaceful state to meet or restart my day and have the strength I need from God to handle whatever the day brings me.

February 9

HEAVEN

Do you ever think about heaven and what it means to you? For me, heaven is not some distant place you go to when you die. Heaven is right here on earth for us all to visit and enjoy...

- Looking into your loved ones' eyes or a child's beautiful face
- Sitting quietly on a gorgeous day enjoying the sounds of the trees whispering in the winds
- On the beach listening to the waves crashing on the shore
- Two friends sipping coffee, enjoying one another's company
- Petting and comforting my dog, feeling her silent love.

These are all examples of finding my heavens as I walk through each day. Anyone can visit heaven at any time. The journey is a thought away. God put nature and other loving souls here for us to enjoy, and it's up to us to find our heavens here on earth. I have found many. What are yours?

February 10

YOUR HEART'S DESIRE

Do you find yourself unhappy with the path you have chosen and want more? At those times, remember, there is greatness within you—it is your heart's desire. Find it, it's there. This greatness is our birthright; God put it there for us to connect with and use to help and heal the world. Let your search begin by taking some time each day to sit and be still, meditating and listening to your inner voice. Allow yourself to let go of all that is and ask in the stillness to be shown what to do, and you will be directed. Perhaps it will be a faint whisper, but if you are still, quiet, and open, your heart's desire will be revealed. This will bring freedom, peace, happiness, and prosperity into your life beyond your wildest dreams and change your life as it has changed mine. God has a very specific plan for each of us that only we are uniquely qualified to carry out. Start listening for your heart's desire today.

February 11

HURT PEOPLE

When we lash out at others, it is often a sign that *we* are hurting inside. Holding in our own frustrations and hurt feelings, rather than discussing them, usually ends in taking out our anger on others. Whenever I find myself acting this way, I am reminded to take the time to examine what I'm feeling. Self-reflection and honesty will uncover why I am lashing out. Usually my hurt and anger have nothing to do with what's going on in front of me at the moment, but it's resulting from something that happened one hour, one day, or one week ago. I have stuffed resentment and negative feelings inside me and lashing out becomes the natural outcome of this behavior. The solution to break free is to talk about it with a trusted friend and bring light to the situation. Then, let it go and make peace with yourself and others. When you no longer hurt, you stop hurting others.

February 12

Radical Forgiveness

Ever wish you could erase your past mistakes? Remember only the good that you did for others? Carrying burdens of your past has never helped you, has it? Then how about if you forgave yourself, forgave everyone else, and hit the reset button? Imagine how peaceful and happy you would be. Start over by forgiving everyone and everything in your past right this second. You only have to make up your mind to do it. It's just a thought away. You will find that the more often you sincerely forgive others, the more you will be forgiven in return. That's how forgiveness works, like a circle completing itself. By extending forgiveness to others, you are guaranteed to receive it when you make mistakes and need it. If we hold it back from others, we withhold forgiveness from ourselves. An attitude of radical forgiveness is very powerful, something I keep in my spiritual toolbox to help me grow and live at peace with myself, God, and others. Forgiving others leads to forgiving yourself.

February 13

PRAYER CHANGES ME

I once heard that prayer is powerful enough to change anything, and so I began to pray. I prayed for my boss to change, my co-workers to change, the economy to change, the weather to change. All these things never came to pass because I had it backwards. Praying to change people and events outside ourselves is futile and will get us nowhere. Changing ourselves to meet the challenges in life is all we can do. Prayer changes me. By using prayer, I can change how I react to other people and the way I view events in my life. My prayers are now simple: when situations arise that are troublesome, I ask God to help *me* change, help me change the way I see people, places, and things, and accept them exactly the way they are. Prayer lifts me above my negative thoughts to view things from a different, higher perspective. By letting go of the idea that I can change anything outside myself, I am returned to peace and changed through the power of prayer.

February 14

START LIVING YOUR DREAM

Live the life you see in your own dreams, not another person's dream for you. Unhappiness, resentment, and misery await if you follow someone else's dream. God did not create us to be stifled by others' agendas. Make up your mind today. Are you a leader or a follower? I woke up one day and realized I was following someone else's dream and made the adjustment to follow my own dream, and my life changed. I want the freedom of doing what's right for me to be happy in this world and allow others their happiness too. No one else is going to fulfill your dreams, only you can do that! Make up your mind right now to chase *that* dream. The way to start is with a plan of action. Take one small step at a time in the direction you seek and start building *your* new future.

February 15

LOOK WHERE YOU ARE GOING

Can you imagine walking around aimlessly without direction? That will only lead you to places you don't want to go. Well, when we speak without thinking first, the same thing happens; we end up somewhere we don't want to be. The consequences of this behavior bring regrets and regrets keep you miserable. The mantra becomes *I wish I didn't say that*, or *I'm so embarrassed by my behavior last night*. Waking up each day with so much remorse on a regular basis because I didn't look where I was going took its toll on me. My unhappiness and depression got the best of me until one day I decided to make changes by watching my thoughts. Taking a moment before I speak and choosing the right things to say assures peaceful interactions with others. Looking where I am going, and acting and speaking accordingly, helps me stay grounded and avoids embarrassing behavior with no morning after regrets.

February 16

IT'S CALLED A TRIBE

There are many people in my life with whom I simply love to spend time. Some are friends, some are relatives, some are co-workers. When we get together, we are able to forget about life's struggles, let loose, and have fun. If I were in trouble, any of these people would be there in an instant to lend a hand; they always have my back. These friendships go beyond this lifetime into others, I'm sure. Our strong bonds are unbreakable. We lift each other up when needed and lend a shoulder to cry on. These precious souls are God's gift to me and what a blessing it is to have them in my life. They are part of my "tribe" and I believe our connection to each other is part of God's plan for my salvation. I appreciate every one of them and am grateful to have them in my life. If you are blessed with supporters like this, nurture them, nurture your commitment to one another, and always be thankful for your tribe.

February 17

THEY WALK AMONG US

They are all different colors, come from all countries, have a lot of money, and have no money. They are bus drivers, salespeople, store clerks, and writers, and they carry messages to us all from God. When we pray for help, they appear. God's messengers walk among us every day. Have you met any yet? Have you been blessed by meeting God's angels? I have met many in my life and continue to meet them. Our paths cross at the exact time we are in need of help and there are no coincidences. These angel messengers of God carry specific messages of hope, protection, and guidance for us. Be open and when you encounter one, listen. Their message could change the course of your life.

February 18

CAN'T OR WON'T?

What's your excuse today? *I just can't get this weight off. I can't quit smoking. I can't find another job. I can't stop drinking. I can't get off these meds.* What does all that "can't" talking really mean? What I have found is that **can't means won't.** The more I dig my heels in and say the word "can't," the more I create a wall of indifference within myself. When I believe that I can't do something, I accept that I *won't* do it. "Can't" sets us up for defeat. "Can't" stops us before we even try to do something or change some circumstance or behavior. You can make an excuse that you "can't" or you *can* make an effort. It's that simple. When your excuses become your mantra, you keep yourself in bondage to the very thing you want to change about yourself. So today, start telling yourself "I can" and God will work miracles in your life. These two tiny words have the power to move mountains. They always do for me.

February 19

DO IT ANYWAY

Each day I put a lot of effort into maintaining my serenity. I take all the right actions to set myself up for peace. I start my day with prayer and meditation to make conscious contact with my Creator. I bless people, ask God to help others, and I remind myself to maintain a quietness and respect for everyone around me. But all those efforts don't always ensure things will go smoothly as the day unfolds. But I do it anyway, knowing a life without God in it is not the way I want to live. I do those morning preparations to prepare me for whatever the day brings. I do it anyway, to remind myself that I am never alone, that God will give me the strength I need to handle whatever comes down the pike. That routine sets the right tone for the day and has become as much a part of my life as brushing my teeth every day.

February 20

TAKE OFF THE CAPE

I sometimes find myself trying to do too many things at once—like trying to shove ten pounds of stuff into a five-pound bag. That's never going to happen. I act as if I'm superwoman and try to defy the laws of the universe. I put on my cape and I step over the line that says *multitask* and go directly to crazy person territory. Why do I do this to myself? It's all a setup. My ego tricks me into thinking I can get everything done in record time and perfectly, when in fact, that's an impossible feat. I'm setting myself up to fail miserably, which will only bring back those old feelings of not being good enough. Once I recognized that I was setting myself up to fail by overfilling my to-do list, I became more realistic. Now I try not to crowd too much into one day. I plan to do only as much as I know I can successfully accomplish without pushing myself over the edge. I take off my cape.

February 21

MEND THAT FENCE

When we hurt others, the right thing to do is to make amends. Once we see our part and that we didn't behave properly, it's time to do the deed. The goal for making amends should always be to clear up our side of the street by taking responsibility for our actions only. A simple "I'm sorry for what I did" is all that is necessary. We don't need to beg for forgiveness. No need to say it more than once or the apology turns to groveling. Making amends can be as simple as this analogy I use: You broke someone's fence. It's your responsibility to fix it since you broke it. Now you must mend it. No need to wait for their approval or even their acceptance. Just go ahead and mend the fence and do not repeat the behavior that got you to this place.

February 22

DON'T GIVE UP, GET UP!

Some days, despite my best efforts, my mind wanders and tries to get me into trouble, like a petulant child stamping her feet, derailing me. Trying to keep this unruly child from acting out takes every ounce of strength I have. Giving up and letting this child have her way often sounds like a good option, but that's when I must stand my ground and *not* give in. This requires a lot of work on my part, but the rewards are worth it. I make the most progress on these days when I don't give up, but *get up*. Instead of indulging my inner two-year-old who is about to throw a tantrum, I resist and stand firm. Resistance is part of growth and without it, you cannot succeed. So, when you're ready to give up, GET UP! Keep moving forward and know you are not only going through it, but you're *growing* through it.

February 23

THE SWEET SPOT

There is a secret place within us that has all the answers to all our questions. I never knew it existed until I searched and was open to believe. This place is our core, the center of our being—which is connected to God—as still as glass and very serene. I call it *my sweet spot*. I visit this place daily and nurture it through prayer and meditation, giving all my worries and needs over to it for the strength and guidance I need in this world. When I reach this place, I'm reaching beyond space and time, and all my cares fall away as I am awakened to the greatness that is within me. I am filled with unconditional love, healing, peace, and gratitude for all. When I receive these glimpses of heaven at my sweet spot, I am taken back to where I came from and will someday return as we are all connected to something much bigger than ourselves. What a blessing to know we each have this sweet spot within us, available for all who seek it.

February 24

I WANT THAT

Why envy what others have and complain about what you don't
have? Plenty of people today are too concerned about what others
are getting. Hey, maybe they earned it. But even if they didn't,
why concern yourself with it? We all come to earth with God-
given abilities and it's up to each of us to discover how to use our
talents, skills, and brains to bring us what we want in our lives. Stop
sitting around wanting what others have and start working hard
for the things *you* want. Look to others not with envy, but with
a sense of "How can I *also* get that?" Most times the things you
want will appear in your life if you work hard. And if you don't get
everything you want, learn to be happy with what you do have, while
continuing to persevere.

February 25

CHARITY DAY!

It's charity day! A reminder to help those who are less fortunate. Clean out your closets and donate items you no longer need that are sitting there collecting dust. There are plenty of people in need of assistance, whether it's your time, money, clothing, or home goods. After all, one person's junk really is another person's treasure. Just think of all the smiles you will put on children's faces by donating your kids' outgrown toys. Or, warm someone up with a coat or jacket that's been sitting in your closet for years. These simple acts of giving go a long way to those who are in need, and your charity will bless not only others, but yourself as well. I am at my best and feeling on top of the world when I give to others, freely. It stirs a gratitude within me for all I have been given and helps me remember where I came from and the others who gave freely to me in my times of need.

February 26

PUT DOWN YOUR SHOVEL

Planning another's demise in my head used to be a big part of my life in the past. When someone offended me, my response was swift and immediate. My mouth opened and out spilled a litany of offenses that would cause others to cover their ears! I reveled in my Jersey girl attitude and after the rampage was over, I felt like a winner. I loved every minute of it and bathed in the glorious success of verbally digging a hole and burying them in it. But, over time, I began to see how the effects of this behavior were toxic to me. Feeding our rage only brings more rage into our lives and nothing good can come from wanting to harm others. So, remember this the next time you find yourself wanting to bury someone—that hole you are digging for someone else is the one you will fall into. Keep your head about you by forgiving the offense. Life is too short and precious to indulge in rage and planning revenge. Put down your shovel and walk away.

February 27

LIGHT YOUR CANDLE

One of the most important lessons life has taught me is that you can't change anyone but yourself. Burn this idea into your consciousness. We cause more harm to ourselves and others by trying to change people and ultimately ruin our relationships with them. Others will be, do, speak, and act as they choose—as we all do. Change can only happen when someone is willing to change. But we can light our candles each day and become living examples of how change is possible through God's miraculous love, kindness, respect, and healing for all. This is how we attract others to want to change. They will see it in us and will want what we have when they are ready to change. So, light your candle each day while interacting with others. Soon, they may see your light spark, igniting theirs.

February 28

PRAY FOR THE WILLINGNESS

Sometimes we try our best and yet continue to struggle. We try and try and then stop when it becomes too difficult and give up. This conundrum, where part of you desperately wants to change yet there is a brick wall around your mind stopping you, is common. This stubbornness causes us to stay stuck and suffer. You want to move past it, but the wall is way too high to climb. Your frustration leads to depression and you feel beaten. Can you relate? Whenever I am of this mindset, the one thing that always works for me is to pray for the willingness. When we pray for the willingness, it's as if God provides the ladder we need to climb over the walls within us and get to the other side. This prayer brings an almighty power to our rescue, which helps us gather the strength we need to overcome any obstacles we face. Pray for the willingness and the ladder appears.

February 29

LEAP FORWARD

Don't look back, the future is ahead of you. Looking back will only cause you to pause. Life is full speed ahead. The frog leaps without even thinking and so can you. Let moving forward become as involuntary as a frog leaping. Go ahead and make your dreams your new reality. Change is imminent when we pursue our dreams with persistence, diligence, and keeping our focus on the next move forward. Ribbit, ribbit.

March 1

THE POWER OF CHOICE

Some bad habits are so ingrained that we continually, unconsciously, act out on them. However, through pain, we are forced to take a look at them with self-honesty. It is then we realize they will never go away on their own and we must take action in order to change. We start by starving them and not feeding them anymore, or we risk falling back into our old ways. By starving a bad habit, we restore the power of choice and only then do we have a shot at changing. God gives you that split second to make a different choice and go in a different direction. This is the grace of God coming to your rescue, helping to release you from the self-constructed prison you have put yourself in. And as we continue to make different choices each day, we experience true freedom from self and are reborn. I thank God for the power of choice.

March 2

WHEN THE STUDENT IS READY

When I was changing my life, becoming sober, and learning to live my truth, I found it useful to explore many spiritual practices, methods, disciplines, and belief systems. My attitude was simple: take what you want and leave the rest. I take any piece of wisdom that speaks to me and try to make it my own. I don't have to follow all the rules. I make my own. You can do the same. Step outside the box and create your own rules. No one has a monopoly on healing, truth, or wisdom. God works through everyone. There's a piece of Buddhist advice that I've found helpful: *When the student is ready, the teacher appears.* Teachers and lessons come to me in many forms, from different people, books, and institutions. The important thing is to be ready to receive, be open to consider what you hear and to learn, being willing to try new things. Keep an eye out for the teachers. When you are ready, they will show up.

March 3

EMPTY TO BE FULFILLED

I have to be emptied before I can be filled or fulfilled. If I'm asking God to help me change some pattern or habit, I have to create a space for new behaviors or ways of thinking. This will never happen with my existing mindset. I must co-create a new one with God. It's the same as when I buy new clothes; I must clear out the closet of some old ones to make room for the new. This morning, I wanted more peace before I left the house, so I stopped watching the TV news and all its negative, fear-based stories. This made room for good thoughts to flood my mind. This simple, practical principle will always work to clear your thinking and unclutter your mind. Make room for new thinking and the new life you want by emptying your mind in order to be fulfilled.

March 4

SMART OR SMARTASS?

We can be smart without being a smartass. There is a big difference between the two and it's all in the delivery and motive behind what you say and how you speak. When we speak from the heart with love and give answers to the questions with love, we are being smart with our words. Conversely, when we want to show off, act like a know-it-all, and try to make others look bad, we are being a smartass. This sarcastic attitude must be tamed in order to have healthy relationships with others. Our words can be hurtful or helpful, depending on how we choose to say them. When speaking to others, nicely say the words you would want to hear. When we come from a place of love, it will always guarantee peaceful conversations and relationships. So before speaking, pause and remember to give others the same respect you would want. Lead the conversation with respect and love for all and be smart, not a smartass.

March 5

WHEAT IN THE WIND

There are lines in my life I will not allow others to cross. These boundaries are for my safety and peace in this world. They involve the way I allow others to speak to me or treat me. I found that when I let others talk down at me or put me down and disrespect me in any way, the line is crossed and the behavior becomes abusive. Allowing this will undermine my security and weaken me much like a wheat in the wind, unable to stand firm. I put myself in this place by not speaking up and enforcing the healthy boundary I've set for myself. Now, I stand up for myself and let others know what's acceptable and what is unacceptable. If you don't say something is wrong, you're saying it's right. Set boundaries and be firm about them—and don't be a wheat in the wind.

March 6

BE A GOOD JUDGE

My judgment of others, when based on their appearances and initial
words alone, is not enough to determine who I will let into my life.
It's only natural that others will always put their best foot forward
initially. My rule is to listen to the words that come next and watch
their follow-up actions to see if they match the first impressions.
Looking past the outside and discovering what's going on inside is
the most important factor as I try to see through the exteriors to
the goodness within them—or the not-so-good—while discerning
who they really are. Ironically, I've found that to be a good judge
of others, you must be free of judgment, and be patient. Only after
you've gathered enough evidence can you make an honest assessment.
The benefits of this patient review are that I have met some of the
most amazing people on this planet, whom I now love dearly, by
withholding a snap judgment. Also, with my newfound discernment,
I have been spared a lot of misery by not allowing untrustworthy
people into my life.

March 7

CLOUDY DAYS

Some days I wake up and am apathetic about everything. I just don't care about anything and want to hide myself from the world. Not a happy place to be. I don't want to pray and feel closed off from my Creator. I feel as though I'm trying to push a giant boulder up a steep hill and it's not budging. These are the days I summon all my will and act *as if.* I start to pray anyway and act as if I *do* care. By sticking with the discipline, I know the urge to pray will return, and after that, the willingness to engage with the world. At those times, I need to remember, God didn't move, I did. Much like cloudy days, the sun is still there behind those clouds and God is still with me and has never left me. I keep the faith, knowing God will show up again just as the sunny, bright days return after the cloudy days.

March 8

DOG IS GOD SPELLED BACKWARDS

Dogs are part of God's kingdom here on earth and are sent to teach us unconditional love. By their loyal and loving example, we can learn a lot from our furry friends. They love us as God loves us, unconditionally. That is why I believe dog is God backwards. When I look into my dog Mollie's eyes, I see pure love without judgment, much like how God loves each and every one of us. She's never in a bad mood, spiteful, or negative—just full of pure love, like a fountain that sends only sweet water, never bitter. Connecting with these beautiful animals is like connecting with God. Owning a rescue dog is one of the most selfless things you can do. We grow closer to God and save an animal who needs a home, while bringing much joy and blessings into our lives.

March 9

DON'T TAKE THE BAIT

On any given day, others may be having a bad day and want to suck you into their misery. Sometimes, knowingly or unknowingly, they will throw bait in the hopes that someone will bite. When you encounter this behavior from others, don't take the bait. It's best to keep peace in your soul by not reacting. Walk away if necessary. If not, and you engage them in their behavior and return fire, expect to go to war. Think about the consequences that will follow. You are sure to become upset and lose your peace of mind and maybe lose a relationship, too. Walk away unscathed by retreating. Save yourself a lot of grief and stress, which can contribute to a plethora of health issues, and steal your peace of mind by resisting that bait.

March 10

STAY IN YOUR LANE

Stay in your lane. Don't try to fix people because you think you know what's best for them. Trying to fix others is control masquerading as "helping others." Unsolicited advice is one of the worst vices in life. It's like driving your car into the next lane and pushing people off the road because you think they aren't driving well. Stay in your lane. Pay attention to your own driving and making sure your own ride is smooth. Others will see this and who knows, they may come asking *you* for driving lessons. That's when your advice will be welcomed and perhaps valued. Being an example is the best way to get others to change without speaking a word.

March 11

INTIMACY

Growing up, I always thought intimacy was something that only happens when you have sex with another person. I thought getting physically naked with another was as intimate as it can get! Once I began my spiritual journey, intimacy took on a whole new meaning and I found it's something much more profound, more than two bodies joining. Intimacy is two minds, hearts, and spirits joining. By letting another person get to know me on a deep, personal level, I have found true intimacy. Being vulnerable by opening myself up and revealing the good, the bad, and the ugly, was one of the scariest and hardest things I have ever done, but this is what's needed to form intimacy with another. The benefits are worth the risks. The experience of allowing someone else to see me on the inside, by taking off all my masks and becoming brutally honest, has helped me accept myself exactly as I am. And by doing so, I have become more comfortable through the discomfort of showing who I am. Real intimacy allows for that discomfort and creates a safe, judgement-free zone with another person.

March 12

LISTEN TO YOURSELF

I always try to form my own opinion of others based on how they treat me, not what I've heard about the way they supposedly treat others. If I find myself listening to your negative version of another person, I will be guilty of contempt prior to investigation. Many times, I have listened to the fray about others without investigation and ruined what could have been a perfectly good relationship. Start listening to yourself. Standing alone and forming your own opinions of others will bring many benefits; I've made several new friendships and lessened the drama in my life by listening to myself instead of others. Reserve your judgment until you have firsthand experience with each new person you meet. Listen to yourself and go with what you know.

March 13

MASQUERADE PARTY

Ever have a day when your thoughts are all over the place? It's as if there are many people stepping forward in your mind and speaking on your behalf. They crowd your thinking, and all want to be heard first. One voice is saying "No" and the other is saying "Yes." Then the angry one emerges, the cocky one speaks, and eventually you don't know what's going on, as if you are at a masquerade party in your mind and you don't know who will show up next. Time to regroup and gather your thoughts. First things first. Quiet your mind and pray. Pray for divine order to flow through your thoughts. This is a powerful affirmation that will get your thinking back on track. By asking for divine order, over and over, even saying it aloud, you will close the door to the masquerade party in your head, letting God guide you back to clear thinking.

March 14

CAN HAPPINESS BE BOUGHT?

What price would you pay for happiness? Would you buy a new home, a new car, a new dress to make yourself happy? Yes, of course, we all do that. Material things sometimes do bring immediate happiness. We pay the price and BOOM: happy. For a time, anyway. But what about longer-lasting happiness, the kind you cannot buy? Like bringing together two people to help them resolve their issues. Or rescuing an abused dog and loving it back to life. Or taking time out to help someone who needs you. These acts of unconditional giving don't come with price tags, but making an investment of your time, love, and skills will transform these acts into lasting happiness. That kind of happiness comes from giving with an open heart and brings a peace in one's soul that doesn't require buying a thing.

March 15

NO STRINGS ATTACHED

Give with an open heart today and expect nothing in return. Go out and give freely of your time, attention, and love to all who cross your path today. Don't ask for anything, just give of yourself. Tell no one about it, keep it between you and God. Work on God's behalf today and watch what you get paid in return. The rewards are astounding. All the petty grievances and concerns in your head will disappear and peace will flow throw you. Giving with no strings attached and when no one is looking is true humility, which feeds your soul and brings you closer to your God.

March 16

WITHOUT NOTICE

Loosen your grips. Don't hold onto people, places, or things too tightly. The universe is constantly changing and so will the circumstances in your life: the only constant in life *is* change. People will move away, jobs will end, relationships will shift. Anything can happen at any time without notice. Your life could change in an instant. So, watch what you are attaching yourself to and remember to keep God first as your source in all your affairs. No matter what changes life sends your way, with God as your source, you will have what you need to meet those challenges and flourish. Never lose sight of your Creator and no matter which way the winds blow, God will be with you wherever you land. Hold on tightly to your faith.

March 17

SLACKING OFF AT HOME

Are you operating at 100%? When things need to be done, do you finish or just get by with half measures? Not sure? Take a look around your home. I know from my own experience that surroundings tell a lot about a person—things like leaving an empty milk carton in the fridge, not replacing the toilet paper, not making your bed, letting dirty dishes accumulate in the sink, allowing weeks of mail to pile up. Sound familiar? These little things we rationalize as "no big deal" often reflect the way a person approaches everything in life. Slacking off at home, doing just enough to get by, and never completing the task at hand is a red flag. This attitude will become your undoing if left unchecked. Eventually, you will do less and less until your home environment overwhelms you. You are cheating yourself and others by just getting by and not giving 100%. (Self-deception has many faces. Say hello to this one.) The antidote is to always give it your all, keeping your living space organized so you can be at peace there. That's right—100%, until completion. This diligence will actually save time, and keeping up after yourself will get easier and easier. The behavior will seep into other areas of life, too, leading to success on all levels.

March 18

VENT BUDDY

There is a way out of every predicament you will face today. You are not alone or trapped. You only feel that way because you are choosing to go it alone, and this is never a good option. Ask for help! Others can help and the solution is nearer than you think. What you need is called a "vent buddy." Someone you can trust who will listen and offer their support. Many times in the past I needed help but never asked for fear of looking weak (which I really was!), and my problems only got worse. Instead of bottling things up inside, dump it all on your vent buddy (with their permission, of course!). After unloading all the misery, you can move on to finding solutions. By asking for help, you allow God's grace into your life and this power will show you the way out of your difficulties by directing you through others. That's how simple the universe works. You have nothing to lose by venting and talking things through. Nothing but your problems!

March 19

RAIN TO RAINBOWS

Rainbows are magnificent creations by God that sometimes emerge after it rains. In my life, many of the meaningful changes were preceded by tremendous pain. I had to go through hell to find heaven: the pains of drinking before I found sobriety, and my most painful experience of hiding my true self before coming out as a lesbian. Embracing the pain led me to a newfound beauty within and I emerged like a rainbow after a storm. Today when I'm faced with pain, I know there is a reason for it and a lesson I must learn. Pain can be a great teacher and motivator; facing it helps me grow, ushers in new beginnings, and brings me closer to who and what I really am. So, embrace your pain and not only go through it, but *grow* through it. Let it rain. Look forward to your rainbow.

March 20

SCARS

Scars on our bodies often tell a story about who we once were and who we are now. What do you think of when you look at your scars? For me, these physical marks show me how God has brought me through some very difficult, painful times in my life by having faith. Some scars are still too new and painful to look at. Others have faded and are easier to think about. My scars are now beauty marks, showing me how strong I have become by reminding me of the pain I had to withstand. I didn't succumb to what was happening to me at the time and instead grew empowered by the experience. My scars are a written testament on my body of how God gave me the strength and healing power to carry on, emerging stronger with more courage and faith to take me to the next lesson life brings.

March 21

SPREAD HOPE

Share your experiences of triumph over adversity. Use them to help and heal others who are going through tough times. This is what our Creator expects of us. Uplift, inspire, and be positive. Many people are hurting and looking for answers and help in this world, and you can be the one to spread a message of hope. There is a big payoff by letting others hear how you have overcome your struggles and bringing them hope. When you do, you elevate your own well-being with new experiences of joy and gratitude for having survived and thrived. Remember where you came from and start spreading hope today, using your own victories over adversity to help someone else get free of theirs.

March 22

DO-OVER

I loved playing sports when I was younger, and I remember certain times during a game when a player or coach asked for a reasonable "do-over." Sometimes we mess up and need to begin again. Such is life. When I miss the mark in life and need to start over, I do the same thing, call for a do-over. No regrets about how I messed up, just do it over again and keep moving in a positive direction for a fresh start. God is waiting for you and is always ready to help you. Life is not about being perfect; we can strive for perfection but will sometimes stumble. That's when you pick yourself up and call a life do-over.

March 23

COME OUT, COME OUT WHEREVER YOU ARE

You never have to run or hide from yourself ever again. I did that for many years and lived a miserable life, embarrassed and ashamed of who I was. I didn't want to be judged or ridiculed, caring far too much what others thought of me, so I hid from the world. But mostly I hid from myself, living a dark and lonely existence. Many times, I even contemplated suicide but through the grace of God, chose to face myself instead. Coming out as a homosexual is a very personal journey. What it came down to for me was, I wanted to live and be free. All the judgment I thought I was going to receive from others never came to pass; the judgment I placed on myself was far worse and that's what was really keeping me in bondage. Now, I know that self-love means accepting who I am, knowing deep in my soul that God loves me and always has. The best freedom is that I no longer care what others think of me and am proud of who I am. No hiding anymore. Telling the truth has set me free and I am at peace.

March 24

ALL IS FUNDAMENTALLY WELL

All is fundamentally well. Say it to yourself, out loud, when fearful, depressed, or just indifferent to what's going on in your life. I rely on this very powerful expression and say it as a prayer every day, to keep away or take me out of negative thinking. No matter what is happening in my life, I keep repeating, all is fundamentally well. Then I add a note of gratitude for all I have so nothing is taken for granted: my sight, my ability to walk and talk, etc. This keeps me from becoming swallowed up by negative thoughts that are swirling around me and recognizing that wellness surrounds me. My mantra reminds me to not let whatever is happening at the moment rule my life. This positive affirmation feeds my soul and is a reminder that whatever I am facing will soon pass.

March 25

RISE UP

Setbacks are inevitable. For every great effort you exert and every aim you put forth to the universe, expect setbacks, even amid positive progress. They come in many guises: health, financial, or anything that stops your flow. But don't fret. Remember, nothing good comes easily and setbacks challenge us to call forth our best. They ask the question, "How bad do you want it?" and force you to look within and dig deeper to achieve what you desire. Don't cave in, because the temptation will always be there to give up, even just as you're nearing your goal. Instead, rise up, take flight, and soar above your setbacks. Your perseverance will bring you to a new state of consciousness and being, living the life you desire and deserve.

March 26

KEEPING ME FIRST

Saying "yes" when you mean "no" is people-pleasing at its best.
We all want people to like us, but people-pleasing can become
an exhausting game our ego plays on us. We can justify this "yes"
behavior by telling ourselves "they need my help" and pushing aside
our own needs. Of course, we should help others but not at the
expense of ignoring our own needs and goals. Continually letting
others' needs take precedence will only create resentment and hurt
feelings, while blaming others for your inability to say no. When this
happens to me, my good deeds are done with a resentful attitude
rather than an open heart; that is not being truly of service to others.
Balance is the key. The importance of self-care and taking care of our
own goals first ensures we can be there for others. As long as your
needs are met first, you will always be acting from a more loving,
caring place within yourself.

March 27

WAITING ON GOD'S WILL

Age-old wisdom says there is a time for everything. You may need to wait a little longer than expected, but your desired outcome may indeed happen. God knows when, and if, you're ready; you don't. Just trust in that; that is all you need to do. Waiting on the will of God can be trying, yet oh so sweet when your awaited outcome arrives. Do yourself a favor and stop knocking your brains against the wall trying to control things. Go with the flow and enjoy the ride. Trust that the right time will reveal itself, that the timing will be what's best for everyone. Once you stop trying to control the timing, you can be present in the moment enjoying life.

March 28

MY OASIS

Life can make you crazy sometimes. Plans go awry and things don't turn out as we thought they would. The events of our life can hurt us, so be gentle with yourself. Take a step back and take care of yourself. Take the vacation, give yourself time to heal, go out with friends, and enjoy life's precious moments. When you need a break from life, follow your instincts, stop everything, and do what you know you need to do. Be with the people who love you and will nurture you. This space you create will become one of your sanctuaries on earth, or as I call it, my oasis in the desert, where I can be me, enjoying the serenity we all crave from time to time. That oasis can heal and will illuminate a better perspective on your life when you return to the tasks at hand.

March 29

CHOOSE YOUR PAIN

Are you unhappy and want to make that change but are scared of letting go? Wanting to change and being able to change is not the same thing, and being stuck in between the two is never easy. We think ahead to the pain and suffering we may have to go through and reason, "Well, maybe it's not so bad after all," and so we decide to stick with the status quo. We do an about face and begin to rationalize our behaviors so we don't have to go through the pain of changing. But, think about this—If your current situation means you are suffering now anyway, why not choose the pain of change? Growing pains have value and will ultimately stop ALL the pain; whereas, sitting with your current conflicts and doing nothing will continue your present circumstances and suffering. Choose your pain! Getting to the other side requires work and some degree of pain but will ultimately bring healing. Which pain do you choose?

March 30

YOU ARE MORE

Grief is heavy. The pain and sorrow I felt when my mom passed away was initially unbearable. It felt as if an elephant was sitting on my chest and I couldn't breathe. We carry grief until it almost swallows us up, then we let it run down our cheeks as tears until we are emotionally drained. Losing loved ones is the worst experience anyone can ever go through. The thought of never seeing that person again is overwhelming, unlike any other pain I have ever experienced. Grief is paralyzing and feels as though it will never leave. But thankfully, it did for me. We do get to the other side of grief, and I found out I am more than the pain. We grow stronger over time by showing up for our lives; the pain of grief changed as I evolved. We will never be fully healed, because a part of us was taken and can never be replaced, but we live in spite of what we feel and go on, making the best life we can, which is what our loved ones would want for us. You will smile again and even laugh when things are funny; that day will come. I've learned that when someone dies, we don't have to.

March 31

No Dumping

There is a huge difference in listening to someone vent versus dumping. Venting is necessary to purge the toxic emotions we feel at times or get clarity on some issue we are facing and is very healthy. Most times after the conversation, we both emerge uplifted and positive, ready to put forth new thinking that was discussed and correct what's wrong. On the other hand, dumping is when someone complains about the same thing, over and over, without trying to fix it and drains us of all positive energy. They suck the life out of us. We all try to be there for others when they need us. But to continually listen to others dump, spewing about the same problem without trying to find a solution is draining. Unfortunately, some people just want to complain, and their negativity will drag you down if you let it. You become an emotional dumping ground for others and may eventually become toxic too. Choose your conversations with others wisely and save your precious energy.

April 1

TOUR GUIDES

To find our way, we all need guides at some point. Someone to show us the way, who can help us navigate our lives, whether at school, at work, or in any new situation. This can be a trusted companion, a way-shower, or what I like to call them, God's angels in disguise. They have been put here by God and show up at the exact moment we need them, preparing the way for us with their guidance. They lead us through the unknown and walk side by side with us to where we need to be. I am grateful for all my tour guides and have become one myself—an awesome job that requires self-sacrifice and commitment, but the rewards outweigh all the work. As I help others, all my needs are met by the paradox of giving to receive. Give back to others what has been freely given to you. Be a tour guide.

April 2

LOOSE GARMENT, NOT STRAITJACKET

Have some fun today. Take off that straitjacket you've been wearing.
Forget about the bills, the raise you didn't get, your long commute to
your new job, and your uncle in the hospital. Chances are, you have
had just about enough of the problems in your life and desperately
need a self-care day, some "me time." Explore things that make
you happy. All your problems will still be there when you return
but you will different. Refresh your spirit and run away for a day.
See a movie, buy that dress, visit a friend and have lunch together.
Whatever it is, just do it. Life is to be enjoyed. Jesus said, "wear the
world like a loose garment," not a straitjacket. Me time turns your
perspective around and restores gratitude for all you have.

April 3

APOLOGY ACCEPTED

Always accept a sincere apology offered by others. To deny anyone who tries to make things right is to deny your own opportunity for forgiveness. It doesn't mean we need to be best friends with the person. We should just acknowledge that they are taking responsibility for their actions and accept their apology. We will all need forgiveness at times in our lives. If we don't forgive, we may not be forgiven when we need it. So, there it is. That's how forgiveness works. If we want to be forgiven, we must forgive others. Forgiveness cleanses my soul and keeps me close to God. We become whole again and have the peace we need to live happy and free.

April 4

FORGIVENESS PRAYER

I've had to forgive a lot people in my life who have harmed me. One of the most difficult ones to forgive was the man who raped me. I wanted him dead, but the pain I wanted to inflict on him was killing me and led me to do many unhealthy things. I was given a prayer many years ago by a very good friend, and it has helped me become free of the toxicity I had built up. By letting go and forgiving, I was no longer a prisoner of my own resentment, setting myself free from the pain I felt inside. I have used this prayer below for all acts of forgiveness with great success, and it has become one of the most powerful prayers in my life. By saying this simple prayer every day, I was able to forgive others and heal myself. No matter what the harm, you will become free too by using this daily prayer. Initially, you may have to recite it through gritted teeth, but as you go along, saying it with sincerity, forgiveness become easier. Then, one day, your heart will link with your mind and you will mean every word! It will lift you above all the hurt and sadness to a new level of consciousness. Place the name of the person you are forgiving in the blank space. Say this prayer once a day.

Forgiveness Prayer

I forgive and release <u>INSERT NAME</u> *from the grip of my resentment now. I give over to God all of the toxic feelings I am harboring and ask to be set free and healed. May* <u>INSERT NAME</u> *find happiness and peace. God bless* <u>INSERT NAME</u>.

April 5

MEMORIES

I love making memories. They last your whole life and can be called upon when you need them to get through tough times or simply when you want to reminisce the good old times. Getting together frequently with my tribe at home has resulted in some of my favorite memories. Dinner parties, barbeques, and nighttime gatherings at the fire pit all bring up a slew of great memories etched in my mind, bringing me so much joy. When I dwell on my own special portfolio of memories from years past, it lifts my spirit. I can mentally flip through them like pictures in a book, reminders of how loved I am and how very special life can be. These memories also get me through the days when I'm missing loved ones who have passed on and the times we shared together, leading me through the grief, finding laughter through my tears. Returning to those wonderful times is only a memory away, giving me great comfort and a sense of peace, soothing and healing my soul.

April 6

SAY THANK YOU

One true path to finding happiness is to be grateful for everything in your life. In the morning, as soon as I awake, I begin saying "Thank you" for all I have. I go through a long list of things I'm grateful for, in succession, not as a rote ritual but offering sincere, heartfelt thankfulness for all God has given me. By doing this, I am creating a space for the universe to flood me with more blessings and this deliberate act of gratitude puts me in a very humble place. I find I attract more goodness while in this mindset and don't find myself wanting anything; I'm just content with everyone and everything in my life exactly the way it is. So, make your checklist and create more blessings, more peace, and more happiness by simply saying "Thank you."

April 7

PROCRASTINATION

I'll do it tomorrow, today was a long day and I'm exhausted. I probably won't get the job anyway so why waste time applying for it. That apartment must be taken, the rent was too good to be true. PROCRASTINATION. We must take a good look at the excuses we feed ourselves when we want to justify doing nothing. When we procrastinate, we let life pass us by. Why do we behave like this? We do it to stay in our comfort zone. Who wants to change, anyway? It's easier to do nothing. Yes, indeed it is, but doing nothing *brings nothing.* You will remain right where you are and watch others fulfill their dreams by venturing out and trying new things. When you procrastinate, you are standing in quicksand, stagnant. Stuck with the same old story you tell your friends, always complaining about your boring life but never doing anything about it. Sound familiar? Then get moving—today. Stop your whining about how miserable your life is and change it now.

April 8

DROPS OF HEAVEN

There are moments I witness in life that bring a smile to my face and connect me with others and the love we all have within. Getting a new puppy, the birth of a beautiful child, kindness shown to others, couples expressing their love for one another. I can't get enough of seeing these manifestations of love. There are also the more intimate moments like witnessing a friend going through tough times and coming out the other side stronger; being there when Cooper, my nephew, says a new word for the first time; the feeling when my dog Mollie stares into my eyes and seems to be looking through my soul, speaking her love to me without words. These are what I call *drops of heaven*. I am overwhelmed with a feeling of love that can only be of God. I am in a special place of time with no fear and complete joy. These moments lift my spirit and when God moments arrive, I savor them and store them in the memory bank of my heart to cherish forever.

April 9

MISTAKES HAPPEN

So, you made a mistake. The world's not going to end. Did anyone die? Unlikely. Are you going to jail for your mistake? Probably not. EASY DOES IT. Let yourself off the hook. Don't be so hard on yourself. You are not perfect and never will be as long as you are in this human state having human experiences. We can strive for perfection and make steady progress, but we falter. As a spiritual being, God has already forgiven you; now forgive yourself. It can be as difficult as you want to make it or as easy as just letting go and starting over. And guess what? You will probably make the same mistake again, but God doesn't care about mistakes, only what we do in response to them. Learning through mistakes is our lifetime job here on earth, so learn your lessons and move on.

April 10

JUST A THOUGHT

What are you thinking about right now? Feeling anxious? What are your thoughts? Most of the time, whatever you spend time thinking about, you will act on. When we take the time to sit quietly and examine our thoughts—instead of letting the day take us over with mental to-do lists, or what our co-worker did to us, or other negative thoughts—we can be proactive about our mental health by replacing negative with positive thoughts. Try it now. Relax and clear your mind of all the mundane worldly chatter. Then, make a mental checklist of things you want to do that are positive—people you want to see, conversations to have, actions to take, friends you can help. By purposely focusing on your thoughts and changing them from negative to positive, you are just a thought away from changing your day.

April 11

TRY SOMETHING DIFFERENT

Don't be afraid to be different. Different is good. Some of us were taught the opposite as children growing up and it's time to change this thinking. Same old, same old is boring, so try stepping out of your comfort zone and take a chance. Whatever it is, push yourself, try another path, explore the unknown. Different actions will bring different results. It's not hard to do, just make the decision. Simply begin by saying "NO" when you mean "NO, or "YES" when you mean "YES." That's a good start. Start being clear about what you want and don't want in your life, and the path will be made clear. One thing is for sure, always expect the unexpected when you try something different.

April 12

COMPROMISE

Compromise is an art that, when practiced, relieves you of stress and anxiety, and restores peace in all your relationships with others. Meeting in the middle is not giving in, it's giving up your stubborn ways and creating an equitable solution for both parties. Practicing compromise has opened doors in my life to new people, places, and experiences that would never have come to pass if I had kept digging my heals in and insisting on my own way. Life is a negotiation and practicing compromise is how we stay at peace with ourselves and others.

April 13

STUMBLE FORWARD

Character building. To me, this is what life is all about. At the end of a long day, it's gratifying to look back and see how we've tried to grow. Simple things like getting to work on time, saying "good morning" to everyone you meet, or helping someone before they ask, allow us to become the best version of ourselves. However, there are days we stumble and are presented with challenges, and we feel as though we are drowning. But, chin up! Pick yourself up, knowing you're still on the path. Even on the days when we miss the mark, we are still learning valuable lessons. We stumble forward. Our mistakes are part of the curriculum and teach us a lot about ourselves. Don't worry so much about stumbling; it's all part of life. Stumble forward and begin again right now.

April 14

LIVE IN THE NOW

Live for right now, because later is not promised. When we put too much stock in what's about to happen later or next week or even next year, or dwell on yesterday, rethinking everything, we miss the beauty of the moment now. Staying rooted in the right now gives us access to our sweet spot, which is where we connect with our goodness, our Creator, our sanity. I can handle anything in the now for it's the only spot in time I can control. Now is the place where I can step out of yesterday's burdens and tomorrow's worries, and put everything in my life into perspective, starting fresh with new ideas and thinking.

April 15

CHOOSE YOUR WORDS

There are a thousand reasons why you should never speak when angry. Our words become toxic and hurtful to others and can ruin relationships. We spew insults and distance ourselves from others and the goodness within. There are no winners when we engage each other in anger; your list of enemies only grows longer. Take a step back, walk away, and think first. Wait until the storm passes so you can talk it over and resolve your differences with the other person in a calm manner. I have learned this the hard way and made many mistakes by talking before thinking about what I was going to say. Now I know that taking the time to consider my words is the easier, softer way. Using restraint to get a point across and be heard without screaming shows tolerance and respect for the other party. Choose your words wisely before you speak and watch how you can turn a situation away from making enemies to living in peace.

April 16

INVISIBLE POWER

Within you lies an invisible power that, when you contact it, will shield you and protect you from harm and help you overcome anything life throws your way. This mighty force can help you walk through your greatest fears with grace and ease, slaying them all. You carry this power within you and connecting with it brings forth the person you always wanted to be but were too scared and weak to become. It is the power of God, which flows through us all whether you believe it or not. When you uncover this force within by having faith in it, expect miracles and watch your life change dramatically. Let the invisible power do for you what you could never do for yourself.

April 17

IF NOTHING CHANGES, NOTHING CHANGES

Have you ever taken honest stock of your strengths and weaknesses?
Most businesses would go broke without doing this regularly. It's
much the same for us people. Taking your own inventory will lead
to making changes in your life, in small and big ways. When you
take inventory, you will find many things that don't belong in your
life—relationships, habits, or situations you've been holding onto out
of fear, need, or because you never saw the negative effects until now.
You will also see where you are making progress and growing. Taking
an honest look at the thoughts associated with what's wrong in your
life reveals the culprits that block your happiness and stop you from
growing. Changing your thinking is important because all change
begins from within. You will attract the same negatives in your life if
your mind is left unchanged. Think about that for a minute. Let it
sink in. If nothing changes, nothing changes.

April 18

LIVE FROM THE INSIDE-OUT

Being afraid and hiding who you are doesn't have to be a life sentence. By letting fear rule our lives, we suffocate on our own wrong thinking and do not live our truth. It's like trying to be vanilla ice cream when you are actually rainbow sherbet. There are many people reading this right now who don't want to talk about, let alone think about, who they are and what's going on inside them for fear of being judged or ridiculed. I know the feeling and suffered for many years until I started living from the inside-OUT and accepted who I am. Whether you are gay, bi-sexual, transgender, etc., you are a perfect creation in the eyes of God and have a right to be here as you are. There are no mistakes in God's kingdom, the only mistakes are the labels the world puts on people they don't understand. We are all on a journey of self-discovery to become the person God intended for us to be, and finding your true self leads to freedoms you never knew existed within yourself. Self-reflection and honesty are crucial and will introduce you to your new self, never having to hide again. You'll become more comfortable in your own skin and find lasting happiness, as it should be.

April 19

UNITY

From my own experience, I can say with all my heart and soul, there is strength in numbers. What I can't do alone, I *can* do with the help of others when we are united for a good cause. Clusters of people with like minds can move mountains together as one. I have seen it happen time and time again. In fact, I belong to such a group of like-minded people and our cause is so strong, we have a collective power that can lift anyone out of darkness and restore their peace. When we gather, God enters into these partnerships, groups, or events that have one goal—love and healing. God pours the strength we need into us when we are acting together out of love and frees us from our fears. I am a living testament of God's strength and power through unity with others.

April 20

STUPID ASS

A very good friend once told me, "When stupid ass knows she's stupid ass, she can't be stupid ass anymore." This statement sounds crude but is packed with meaning. I see this as an empowering, if somewhat comical statement for times when you recognize your own destructive behavior and sincerely want to change. I took those words and started applying them to my own life. The first order of business I needed to change—the first way I was being a stupid ass— was allowing people to take advantage of me. I was always leading with an open heart, doing too much for others and I found there are people in this world who look for kind-hearted unsuspecting people they can take advantage of and hurt. I woke up finally, smelled the coffee burning, and learned that all my relationships must be on a give-and-take basis. Healthy relationships reside in the middle somewhere. Waking up and recognizing when you are a stupid ass is the touchstone to freedom and brings much peace.

April 21

KINDNESS IS LOVE IN ACTION

There are many aspects of what God is to me though this changes as my understanding grows. To me, the most important, constant aspect of God is love, which manifests in many ways. One is kindness. The path of kindness is love in action—soothing, healing, and emanating from within us all. Kindness can be tapped anytime we choose. Being kind to others is an expression of love which is of God and showing kindness to every living creature is God's will. We are ambassadors of God's love and our life's journey is about finding that power within us and using it on His behalf. Kindness heals and help others. I have found my inner power when I put forth kindness in any situation, and then I'm blessed beyond comprehension. This is doing the will of God and pays huge dividends when practiced daily.

April 22

SETBACK OR COMEBACK?

Having a setback today? Did your plans go awry and things didn't turn out the way you expected? Don't fret. Behind every setback is a comeback waiting in the wings. The trick is to accept that whatever you were hoping for was not meant to be at this particular time for some reason and know that God has something much better in store for you. So, pick yourself up and start over. See this experience as a stepping-stone to something much better and begin your comeback. Keep a positive outlook and expectation of good things to come while persevering until your goals are achieved. Turn your setback into a comeback!

April 23

MAKE YOUR BED

Do you make your bed? Making my bed is a daily discipline that I began years ago on the advice of a friend. She told me if I was ever going to change, it would mean changing everything. How could I ever expect to find the strength to overcome something difficult if I can't even commit to doing something simple like making my bed? So, I began doing it, and to this day I haven't stopped. What I have found is that when you must change, doing the opposite of what you've done before is how to make a new person, step by step; doing the simple things add up to big changes in ourselves. Making my bed, along with other daily disciplines, especially prayer and meditation, helps pave the way for God's power to flow into my life. This feeds the spiritual warrior, giving me the strength I need to change and handle life on life's terms. Each day I measure my willingness to work on myself by this daily discipline and when I don't feel like making my bed, I make it anyway as part of my commitment to myself. And it also keeps my house tidy!

April 24

INTERNAL COMPASS

Once you've set your heart on some course of action or goal, don't waver in your plans. Stay focused and don't get lured off track by thinking maybe there's a better or easier way. That is how our ego keeps us confused and off balance. If you've found the solution, run with it and stay true. I quit smoking, thankfully, by choosing and sticking to a plan of action and have not had a cigarette since 1997. God gave me the willingness and the idea of how to quit, and I followed that plan to the letter. Once God puts an idea in your head, it's a gift; embrace it and guard it against detours or detractors. Your intuition and intention combine to form a powerful internal compass that connects you to the power of God and will lead you to success. That compass is always telling us the right thing to do. So, sit quiet, listen, and follow.

April 25

EATING FOR COMFORT

Do you eat because you're hungry or do you hunger to eat? The two are miles apart. Eating because you are hungry is what humans must do to survive. The other is eating for comfort, which can become an addiction if unchecked—something I found out for myself when I realized I was taking comfort by eating. That kind of addiction can kill you if you indulge long enough. I had to learn to recognize the point when my body is full and does not need any more food. At one time, I'd I continue to eat anyway. Now I know there is a direct link between overeating, heart disease, diabetes, and other health problems. Using food for comfort may be very subtle and hard to identify yourself. I've learned to notice that when I have a bad day, I want a reward, or when things go wrong and I want to feel better, my first inclination is to fill the emptiness within me with food. Boredom is another time when I might overeat. Now, when I do spot these feelings and behaviors, I ask God to help me with this prayer: "Lord, let food fill my body, but You fill my soul." Remembering always that God can do for me what I cannot do for myself helps me close that refrigerator and reach for something else—like a good book or a walk in the park.

April 26

No Conforming

I don't want to be put in a box as a person or as a writer. I am who I am and will not conform to what society expects. For me, love is the only rule to follow. To think, speak, and act with love can only produce a successful outcome. I write with the intention of helping others better understand themselves and their relationship with God and finding peace. What I write may not "color within the lines" nor conform to many of the world's rules. That's okay; I make my own! Be who you are and you will never have to explain yourself. If you find yourself constantly trying to explain, keep it moving; you have not yet found your audience. We all have special gifts and talents. Celebrate your uniqueness and never apologize for who you are.

April 27

A GREAT MIND

When I'm around negative people, I sometimes can get sucked into their abyss and become negative too. I begin to take others' inventory and when I find myself doing this, I notice it feeds my superiority complex and I start comparing myself to others, pulling them down to make myself look better. It's a great day when I catch myself doing this and I can start my day over right then and there. Turn the negative around into positive by remembering no one is better than anyone else. A great mind is a mind that can change when it needs to. When everyone around you is talking trash about others, walk away and stay focused on putting positive thoughts into your mind. You will start attracting people who feel the same way and will restore peace and goodwill to yourself and all who you meet.

April 28

SURRENDER TO WIN

Surrender does not mean we give up, but we *give over* to something greater than us. I used to think surrendering was a sign of weakness but today for me, it's a very brave spiritual act. When I surrender, I get clarity and the madness stops. Whatever it is that is causing me harm or concern, I give the worry over to God and the miracle of healing always begins. Surrender is the prerequisite for change, but first I must sacrifice my will and control of the situation, letting it all go before I can become new. I must be emptied of all my thinking so new thinking can enter. Surrender is the first step in changing my thinking and when my thinking changes, my behaviors change.

April 29

COMPASSION MAKES AN APPEARANCE

Thinking about compassion doesn't make you a compassionate person nor does talking about it. Stepping up and helping others in need without being asked is compassion. When compassion wells up within and makes its appearance, we then must make a conscious decision to act on it. Helping the lady at the grocery store who dropped her bags all over the floor is compassion. Listening with an open heart and without judgment to a friend who is having a difficult time is compassion. Bringing a meal to someone who is sick or driving them to a doctor's appointment is compassion. Compassion, usually coupled with kindness, is love in action. Extending selfless love and kindness to others, expecting nothing in return with no strings attached, is compassion. It's that simple. Take time today to perform an act of compassion for another. The benefits are peace, happiness, and gratitude for all you have.

April 30

LISTEN WITH OPEN HEART

A friend called the other day and was very upset. I listened and patiently let him get out all his frustrations, knowing that holding them in will lead to more stress for him. I let him vent and get the clarity he needed to be restored to calmness. Whenever I am listening like this to a friend in pain, I am also silently praying for him, asking God to let me be a channel of healing and help. Once my friend was done sharing his burden, he sounded a bit lighter and I heard in his voice how much he needed to share his worry. Sometimes that's all it takes, to listen with an open heart—no advice, no solutions— just being there for someone, listening. Others have done the same for me many times, so I always reciprocate. We both end the conversation feeling refreshed, clear of purpose, and filled with an inner strength once again. Listen to others so someone will be willing to listen to you one day when you need an open heart.

May 1

FIND THE LESSON

There is always a lesson in everything that happens in our lives. Whenever there are changes happening in my life, I find myself walking around asking myself *Why now? Why me?* The question I should be asking is "What's my lesson?" I believe that everything happens for a reason, so if we can get through the "Why me?" to "What's my lesson?" we are on our way to understanding the reason. This is the game changer for me. Then, it's on to better days and the healing begins. When a relationship with a so-called friend ended, it turned out to be a blessing in disguise. Moving past the initial shock, I began to look for the positive lesson in what happened, which was to follow my gut instincts and not allow untrustworthy people in my life. When your gut tells you something or someone isn't right, listen to it and more importantly, act on that information. I find our lessons can come in many guises, some less painful than others, but we trudge on nonetheless staying positive, awaiting another new beginning to a happier, healthier life.

May 2

It's Called a Conscience

Everyone knows the difference between right and wrong. We all have that still, small voice within us that speaks up right when we're going to do something we shouldn't do or not do something we should. That voice is called our conscience, a spiritual connection to the universe filled with ethics, morality, and integrity. Our conscience is always speaking to us, and having one is what connects us to God. It's the voice of reason we hear when we argue over petty nonsense, telling us to forgive and love each other. Or, the voice that tells you not to blame others for your shortcomings but to look at yourself and take responsibility for your part. But do we listen? Sometimes yes, sometimes no. I find when I do listen and act from what my conscience is telling me, my life seems to flow free and easy and all is well. All my needs are met and yes, some of my wants too. Whenever your conscience talks, do listen. It has something very important to say and will always guide you to your highest good in all situations.

May 3

GET EVEN, GET EVEN, GET EVEN SICKER

The price we pay for getting even is…we get even sicker. Holding on to the hurt we experience in life and that desire to get even with others has major consequences. By planning to hurt others, we only hurt ourselves. We keep toxic emotions within us and become sick. We get even, get even, then get even sicker! No matter what was done to us, real or imagined, carrying this burden will only keep us sick and miserable. The remedy is to forgive. It feels like you are giving in to the other person, conceding to them. But just the opposite is true. When I let go and forgive, I free myself from the bondage of anger I am carrying for another person. Instead of continuing to feel badly and plotting how to get even, I give up the hurt and empty myself of negativity so I can begin my healing. As I forgive others, I am forgiven for my mistakes too. Forgive and you are forgiven. Love and you will be loved. And so it goes.

May 4

WORD VOMIT

Sometimes we speak way too much and it becomes difficult for others to listen to us. We test others' patience by trying to sound smart, throwing up words about topics we really don't know anything about, talking incessantly just to hear our own voice! We talk a lot but say nothing. This is what I call "word vomit." It is quite the turnoff, and no one wants to listen to it nor should they. I have found that when we speak, less is more. Getting our point across does not require a diatribe of verbiage, just clear, honest, and concise words that touch the main points. Honestly speaking from your heart hits the other person's heart, while speaking from your tush… well, you get the idea. Word vomit is a symptom of an insecurity within that manifests as uncontrolled talking about nothing and hurts the listener's ears. When you find yourself doing this, stop— and give yourself as well as others a break.

May 5

KARMA

It's my belief that there is goodness in the universe and that there is
no such thing as a punishing God, only a loving one. God is love
and only love can come from this mighty power, not punishment.
Punishment does come to us, however, as consequences for our
actions. This is what the Buddhists believe and call the law of Karma.
There are invisible laws of the universe that God created to preserve
our free will, and Karma dishes out consequences for our actions in
an impersonal way. No matter who you are, if you break the laws,
you will be met by consequences for your actions. No one gets
around it, whether you believe in Karma or not. Just like touching
a hot stove will bring pain as a consequence or if I was to walk off
a rooftop, I would fall to the ground like a rock due to the law of
gravity. Once I accepted these ideas, the more responsible I became
for my actions. Having a better understanding of Karma means I
consider my actions, and this has improved my life.

May 6

MIND ARCHITECT

What do you want to be? Who do you want to be? We have the power to manifest whatever is in our minds, and the thoughts we think bring us to the destination we envision. Let your thoughts pave the way to the new you. Be the architect of your mind and plan your new beginning. Don't hurry, don't worry about it being too late; each day is a new beginning. Start now and let time serve your highest good by using it wisely instead of letting it pass you by. Create the person you always wanted to be with your new blueprint. Make love your blueprint, love for God, for yourself, and then for others. When you put your life in that working order, expect to be introduced to the person you always wanted to be.

May 7

PERSEVERANCE

If you have been working hard to change something about yourself and are at a standstill, you are actually right where you should be. Change is hard and there will always be roadblocks along the way, but the struggles and plateaus that are part of change won't last forever, as long as you persevere and keep moving forward. Your long-awaited day of reckoning and payoff will be here before you know it and you will be brought to a new level of thinking and being. The joy is in the journey and sometimes the journey is long and hard, and there are delays, but the rewards are oh so sweet. Success always comes to those who make the commitment to do their best every day, and never give up. Keep your eye on the prize and remember the reasons why you started on your new path. You were sick and tired of something in your life and made the decision to change. Whatever the reason, be proud of yourself for trying to become the best person you can be by persevering through the tough spots.

May 8

YOU ARE NEVER ALONE

Even when you're by yourself, you are never alone. Whether you believe it or not, you are always connected to the most powerful power in the universe—a mighty force that created, loves, and protects you. And making contact with it each day is the most important thing I can do for my spiritual health. I call that the power God, and it speaks to me through my conscience when I quiet myself during morning prayer and meditation. This act centers me and prepares me for the events of the day ahead, reminding me of who I am and who walks with me as I go through my day. While I may be on my own, I am never alone. God is with me. Like the ever-watchful eyes of a parent on their child, God is watching over me.

May 9

NEGATIVITY BREEDS NEGATIVITY

Sometimes we don't have a choice and find ourselves in the company of negative people with negative energy. You know who I'm talking about—people who seem to think they know it all. They talk over you. They never let you speak nor do they listen. They complain about others, not treating them fairly, ad infinitum. They are blinded about themselves and want to point the finger at others, blaming everyone for every little thing that is wrong in their lives and cannot see that they are the problem. If you recognize this person, keep a healthy distance. Their negative energy will become your negative energy if you stick around too long. Negativity breeds negativity. If you hang around the garbage can long enough, you'll start stinking like the garbage. Being around negative people is something none of us can avoid, but when I sense negative energy around me, I say a prayer and remove myself as quickly as possible.

May 10

TRUST ME

From my experience, the only way to gain another's trust is to be honest. Start being your true self, whoever you are at this moment, and be honest in all interactions. With no pretense, others will see your sincerity. At one point in my life, I had to earn back the trust of my family, employers, and friends, a huge task that took time. But I accomplished it with sincerity and honesty in all my affairs and I am now proud to be called trustworthy. Honesty is like a magnet that pulls trust directly to it. Honesty and trust go hand in hand; you can't have one without the other. To be trusted, I had to be the same person at home, at work, and with friends and always be truthful. As you become more honest with others, trust is the natural outcome.

May 11

WHAT MAN REMOVES, GOD REPLACES

Whenever I feel cheated out of something I deserve and have worked hard for, my first reaction is to meet these situations with resentment. I then become depressed, convinced that people are getting something over on me. This attitude creates a wall within me that is impenetrable. While it's there, no success can arrive and nothing good can come into my life. I had to find another way to think or I would be spending my life letting people live rent free in my head and never having the success I deserved. I had to begin forgiving others and start depending on God as my source, knowing no one can ever take from me what is rightfully mine. My new prayer and mantra became "*What man removes, God replaces.*" Try saying it over and over until you mean it and it sinks into your DNA. God will open another lane and replace what was lost with something better. I don't have to struggle to get what's mine. With God as my source, nothing can ever separate me from my good except my own limited thinking.

May 12

SLIGHTS ARE TERMITES

A slight from another can turn into a war when we allow it to burrow within our minds, much like termites that, unchecked, will devour a home over time. Over the years, I ended up quitting jobs, leaving relationships, and retreating in some way when I allowed a slight to affect me, and thus lost many opportunities because of my pride. Well, you don't have to let it go this far. When you're at the receiving end of criticism, gossip, or hurtful comments, best to talk it over with a trusted friend so the hurt doesn't fester and become a huge resentment. Then let it go. There will always be people in our path who say and do things that are hurtful or not true. Don't buy into the nonsense. Remember, when you do, you allow termites in and these petty nuisances must be avoided if we want peace.

May 13

MARTYRDOM

It takes great courage to become a martyr. Giving your life over to save or help others for a just cause is the highest sacrifice and I have deep respect for true martyrs. Their motives are pure and of God. Many throughout the course of history have made an important difference in the world by their selfless sacrifices and I am deeply grateful to them all. But I want to speak of another kind of martyrlike sacrifice, which has its roots in feeding the ego: people who want to sacrifice and suffer only to look good in the eyes of others. This is a self-serving act of cowardice, miles apart from true martyrdom. Remember the difference. When your motive is to please yourself and look good to others, this is feeding your ego. If you are going to sacrifice for the good of all, do it not for yourself, but to make a difference in the world. That is how we aspire to true martyrdom.

May 14

WHAT DID YOU SAY?

Who you are is evident the moment you enter a room. We wear our personalities on our chests. If you are struggling because you think people don't like you or they don't get your personality, maybe it's time you took a good look in the mirror. Who is looking back at you? Face it, can everyone else always be wrong? I don't think so. If you continue to get critical feedback, instead of blaming others, ask yourself what you are doing or saying that causes this reaction. Through thoughtful introspection, find the person you really are by taking an honest inventory. Most times we are blinded by pride and cannot see ourselves as we really are. We may need the help of a friend to help objectively point out the things about us that we need to work on, which is essential to get to the truth. Ralph Waldo Emerson (1803–1882) said,

"Who you are speaks so loudly, I can't hear what you're saying." When the same old, same old issues become a pattern in all your relationships, it's time to examine how your behaviors are sabotaging you and if they need an overhaul. Look to yourself first, if you expect to find your peaceful place among others.

May 15

HELP SOMEONE, HELP YOURSELF

Healing from your past is a process, and before it happens, layers of hurt and grief must be sifted through and reconciled. This takes time and patience with ourselves and does not happen overnight. While I am healing, I find doing for others gets me out of my own pain. I'm no longer thinking about my problems but helping you with yours. I entrench myself in what I can do for you and how I can alleviate your suffering. When I help someone else, I help myself. This paradox can be your saving grace, passing along to others the valuable lessons you have learned, helping them in their struggles. Let God use your struggle to heal as a way to help others and you will always emerge stronger than ever!

May 16

THE COWARD MAKES THE BULLY

When others continually say negative, hurtful things about you and you do nothing, a damaging dynamic in relationships is set in motion. By accepting the bully's aggression and lies, your inaction gives your consent, empowering the bully to continue. As your insecurity grows, you have a hand in the ongoing bullying situation! Hence, the coward makes the bully. Both are affected by this dynamic. One is empowered, the other is derailed. But just as you put yourself in the position, there is also a way out. You can take back your power by standing up for yourself and breaking the cycle. Do you really want to give power over yourself to others? Release your fear and the next time you are feeling bullied, remind yourself "the coward makes the bully." Standing up for ourselves is the only remedy when we are bullied by others.

May 17

IT'S NOT BIGGER THAN GOD

From my experience, everything I always wanted lies on the other side of fear. Fear is the stumbling block we all meet at some point in our lives and can be paralyzing at times. Today, don't let fear dictate how you live. Start anew and choose courage over fear. You can be free of fear or you can live in bondage. You have a choice. It's that simple. When we choose courage, we choose the power of God which is bigger than anything. Pray and walk on and through whatever it is you are afraid of, that's what you do. Do it over and over until you drive the fear out! Like an unwanted guest in your home, cast it out! Tell yourself continually: IT'S NOT BIGGER THAN GOD! When I walk through my fears with God, my whole being changes and I am filled with courage beyond words. I am lifted up by my faith and no longer afraid, gaining strength for the next obstacle life will put in front of me. Courage dispels the lies we have fed ourselves and shows us we can do or overcome anything with God.

May 18

DOING THE DO

Need a sign that you are on the right path? Keep looking because it's coming soon. Continue doing the do. Some days are a process of waiting; you must wrestle with your faith and endure. You come very close to giving up, but reconsider. Just like when you get up and start the day instead of pulling the covers over your head and staying in bed, you keep going; you get up, suit up, and show up, holding fast to your faith when everything around you is uncertain and changing. Doing the do gets you through. It can be a rough ride having to wait patiently but then the sign appears. You emerge with more faith than ever before and are grateful you stuck it out instead of selling out.

May 19

REDEMPTION DAY

Your best days have finally arrived. Here they are! All the hard work you've put in for so long now, and finally—BOOM! All your dreams are coming true! It's redemption day and you deserve all your good fortune. Whether it has to do with health, finances, or a relationship, the reward has finally come full circle. What a blessing. Give thanks to your Creator and enjoy your newfound happiness. Living our dreams and finding our heart's desire is our birthright, allowing us to live our highest good, which is heaven on earth. Revel in your blessings from all your hard work. You deserve all the goodness that has been brought into your life!

May 20

LOVE YOU, MOM

Today's message is inspired by my relationship with my late mother. Today is Mom's birthday and I am filled with her memory. But these words are for anyone who was raised by a special person, whether it's your grandma, sister, father, or brother. You will certainly identify with the love and connection we shared.

Mom brought me here to this world. Selflessly, out of love, carried me for nine months, watching me grow and fiercely protecting me. As the years moved on, she stayed by my side throughout the good and the worst times of my life, always my cheerleader. I cherish the wonderful memories that bring tears to my eyes when I think of how much fun we had together. The memories are etched on my soul and will remain with me always. The deep connection we shared in life and even through her death will be with me throughout eternity, a bond that will never break. I am part of her and she is part of me and we will always be together in spirit. Some days I can still feel her presence with me. I may never be able to physically hold her or touch her again, but my memories will always comfort me. I love you and miss you, Mom. Thank you for the love and support we shared together…until we meet again.

May 21

TAKE IT OR LEAVE IT

Take what you want and leave the rest. You don't have to follow every piece of advice you hear or do what seems to work for others. There are many ways to achieve your goals; the world is a vast planet with many resources to choose from. So many tools are available. Sort through them all, then pick the method that suits you and stick to it until you see the results you want. If that does not work for you, try another approach, but don't quit altogether. The key to change is being willing. Once the willingness arrives, you will ultimately succeed with whatever method you choose. The willingness to want to change anything in our lives is what brings us to our goals.

May 22

WANT OR NEED?

We've all heard the saying, "Be careful what we wish for, it may come true." If we don't think it through, wishing for things we don't have can sometimes bring unexpected consequences. Over the years, I've wanted so many things but when they arrived, I wasn't ready, and it caused me a lot of unnecessary problems. Now, when I want something, I do an honest check of my motives first. Ask yourself, "Do I want it or do I need it?" (Most times you will stop right there.) If we are honest with ourselves, it will become clear instantly if it's a frivolous want or a legitimate need. When it's a legitimate need, I put it in God's hands, asking for guidance and wait on the results. If it's meant to be, it will be.

May 23

WORK IN PROGRESS

Begin again, that's all you need to do. Mistakes happen, that's why there are erasers on pencils. We aim to do good and sometimes we fail. Starts and stops are a huge part of growing and no one gets it perfect on the first try. God has created us perfect in our souls, but we are imperfect in our human bodies. We are perfectly imperfect. We aim for perfection and walk in that direction, but stumble. That's how we grow spiritually. We are all a work in progress, always striving to be our best. That's all God expects of us each day.

May 24

DEFLECTION IS DECEPTION

Blaming others and playing the victim is easier than looking at ourselves. It's deflection that causes deception in our thinking. The blame game begins with that quick, automatic decision we make when things go wrong in our lives and we say, "It's not my fault." At one time, this blame reaction was embedded in my brain and it took me a long time to see how this delusional thinking crippled me. By not taking responsibility for my actions, it ruined relationships and kept people away, leaving me feeling alone and wondering why. It was only when I began to be honest with myself, see my part in situations, and take full responsibility for what I had done or not done that I was able to restore and enjoy my relationships. Now, self-honesty keeps me awake to situations that may tempt me to blame others. Instead, I keep the focus on myself.

May 25

ENVY

I never thought of myself as an envious person until I became irate watching others succeed and wanting what they had. I always attributed it to my competitive nature kicking in, but life is not a competition. When I find myself wishing for what others have, I generate a negative energy called ENVY, which will never attract anything good into my life. As a matter of fact, just the opposite will happen. When we're envious, we push away the very thing we want. The only remedy is to be thankful for everything you do have and wish the same for others. This thinking will create and attract abundance and blessings in your life by showing your appreciation to God for all the gifts given to you. When I put forth this positive energy, and pair it with working hard, setting goals, and being true to myself, I will attract whatever it is I want into my life. This is the true key to abundance.

May 26

ARE YOU HANGRY?

Whoever said not eating properly can affect your attitude? It's true. Running around doing errands and chores at 100 miles per hour while not eating properly makes you angry and causes the phenomenon known as "hangry"—hungry *and* angry. When your patience is withering, your stomach is growling, and you're not achieving the tasks you set out to do, you're hangry. The anger within is brewing and the next person who crosses your path is going to get your wrath. Those in recovery from addiction or eating disorders know the answer is to stop and call a HALT before someone gets hurt. HALT stands as a reminder to ask yourself if you are hungry, angry, lonely, or tired. It's a handy acronym whenever any of those feelings get you stuck. HALT and replenish. Stop, eat, rest, and your perspective changes. Once you meet your body's needs, you will have returned to sanity.

May 27

SHAME

Feeling shame about your past can be cured by forgiving yourself. I felt shame about things I wish I never said or did, and it made me want to crawl into a hole and hide from the world. I remember once being at a supermarket and seeing a person from my past, bringing up bad memories I thought were forgotten. The pain I caused this person, without them even knowing, made me feel awful. As bad as I felt, I needed to feel those emotions in order to change. It forced me to see my part and take responsibility for what I had done. By making my amends and not repeating the same behaviors, I began to heal and forgive myself. In this way, I have found shame to be a very good teacher, showing me what I need to change so I do not repeat past behaviors. By choosing to do the right thing in my life, I distanced myself from the person I was by making better choices in thoughts and actions, thus forgiving myself and banishing shame.

May 28

HOW RICH ARE YOU?

How do you measure your worth? Money and popularity? Possessions and property? Much of the world thinks this way, and some of us have been brought up believing this. But money and material things are fleeting. You really can't take it with you, and I don't want to be the richest person in the cemetery, leaving a legacy that is nothing more than a bank account balance. Your real value has nothing to do with any of these things. Our real value comes down to one thing: how much love we give in the world. Do you sacrifice your time to help another? Unselfish acts and deeds create your worth in the eyes of God and your fellow human beings. I may not have a dime in the bank, but I have stored up riches and blessings in the bank of heaven. Accumulating money is useful, but the love given to one another here on earth is the only thing that determines our value in the end.

May 29

SPEAK FROM LOVE

Whenever someone asks my advice, my first response is to pray to be a channel for God's words to flow through me. We are all channels for God's words and will be used to deliver messages to those who suffer. You don't have to be a great orator; we all have the ability to speak in small, honest, gentle ways that can help others. If someone is seeking your advice, just be willing and pray to be a channel and God will put the words in your mouth. Then remember to speak with love, for love heals and that's what's needed when someone is hurting and needs direction. Sometimes you must tell someone the truth about an issue and that message may be difficult for them to hear, so we need to be cautious and kind about how we deliver it. Our words may be the very thing that saves their life! Speaking truth without love is cruel but withholding truth can be cruel as well. Speak from love and be a healing channel of God's expression.

May 30

THE GREAT COVER-UP

For most of my life, my perceptions of reality were way off. I would either minimize and rationalize my problems or blow them up into spectacles that created more drama than any TV soap opera. When problems arose, the pendulum would swing and I never knew where it would stop. This self-deception was ingrained in me and distorted my way of thinking, causing me to deflect everything onto others so I wouldn't have to look at myself and take responsibility. It was the great cover-up. Pretend everything is okay. Pretend all will be fine. Truth is, everything was falling apart. I was in denial and covering up. Denial, when left unchecked, ultimately leads to self-destruction. We all succumb at times to denial, so we must be vigilant against the lies we tell ourselves. Our minds can deny, rationalize, and cover up anything. Stay awake each day and watch your thoughts. That is where the fairy tales we tell ourselves begin and start a life of their own.

May 31

BE A LIGHTHOUSE

A lighthouse helps ships at sea navigate, sometimes leading them to shore when they are lost or in need of assistance. The lighthouse beacon lets floundering vessels know that help is nearby and how to safely reach port. We are sometimes like a storm-tossed boat, lost and searching for a protected harbor; we need a beacon of hope to guide us back to safety. There were many people who were my lighthouses, guiding me back to sanity. Their comforting words gave me hope and I will always be grateful to them all. Now, I try my best to be a lighthouse for others and let my light shine out to all who have lost their way. In this way, I can spread hope, guidance, and love to all who are in need. Because others were there for me when I was searching for a safe port, I will always return the favor with pleasure. We both emerge blessed by God and can create more beacons of hope for others. Be a lighthouse.

June 1

I Know...

Being full of yourself is dangerous. When I think I know it all, I stop learning. Instead, being open and remaining teachable has been my saving grace. To be teachable, first we must be emptied before new knowledge can enter our mind. I now begin new encounters with a silent reminder to myself: "I *don't* know." This makes so much sense before starting anything I'm not familiar with or entering a situation with which I have no experience. This clears away any residual tendency to think I know more than I do and gives me a new perspective and reference point so I can begin learning something new. This attitude of being teachable assures that I'll always have a flow of interesting new knowledge coming into my life to help me grow. Stay teachable. Remember what you don't know.

June 2

SPIRITUAL GPS

When something unexpected happens is it really an interruption or does God have another plan for you? We've all had the experience of moving ahead, everything in place, then plans suddenly go sideways. "Now what?" you ask in frustration. Diversions and curveballs in life are God's detours and happen sometimes in an instant. This is the time to get your spiritual GPS ready. God is rerouting you for a reason, and ultimately the outcome is in God's hands. You are being called to trust and accept the situation exactly as it is. Just like entering an address in our car's GPS, we let go and drive, letting the directions lead us to our destination. It is the same with our Creator. Go with the flow and keep the faith until you arrive at your new destination. Give thanks for having a loving, protecting, higher power who will always guide you to safety.

June 3

WORK HARD, HARDLY WORK

Do you work hard or hardly work? We all have days when we do one or the other—and sometimes both on the same day. Some days I glide through my work tasks and some days I trudge along. The days I trudge are the "piano on my back" days. Every little thing I must do feels like hard work. Other days, I glide along, accomplishing even complicated tasks with ease. That's when I know my spirit is directing me; those days never feel like work, but happily finding my place and settling into it. When work flows effortlessly, I experience a true joy. I am in that space and time which is of God. I am right where I'm supposed to be and nothing can touch me. Effortless thinking, doing, and being. My kind of work.

June 4

CAN YOU IMAGINE?

I'm a believer that we were all created under one God and are all brothers and sisters in spirit; yet at the same time, all of us are different. Our differences are what make us unique and being different should not mean we are outcasts but only that we bring special qualities unlike what others can offer. There is enough room in our world for us all to be who we are, without judgment, and get along despite our differences. We can find the place where we can all come together and treat each other with love and compassion, starting with each one of us, right now. You see, it's all how you perceive your fellow human beings. Focusing on what we all have in common rather than our differences will help us create a world in which we can all be free and live peacefully. Let's start today and we can change the world! Can you imagine?

June 5

START SAILING

Sit and think about this for a minute. Who do you want to be? You have the power within you to become whoever you decide. Pretty powerful, huh? Well, it's true. Conjure up the person that you want to be in your mind and then step into the part. You have a choice. Becoming who you want to be all begins in your mind. Behind every action is the thought first. Set your intention to the universe as a boat captain sets his sails on his vessel and then travel ahead in that direction. Sail on to your destination with a new sense of purpose and become all you ever wanted to be. You can chart your own course in this life. God has given us free will to choose who we want to be. Visualize what you want to be, think it, act it, and finally, become it.

June 6

GIVE A LITTLE, GET A LOT

Sometimes, it seems everything in this world has a price tag attached. *How much is that item worth? What does it cost? What will I get out of that experience?* Ever try doing something without thinking about costs, monetary, or what's in it for you? Just to help another person? Giving freely without expecting anything in return is an art that pays very well. I'm not talking about giving away your paycheck; we all need money in order to survive. I'm talking about giving of yourself, your time, and talents, and expecting nothing in return. By giving to others we increase what we have, reaping intangible rewards. God pours his blessings into us when we give of ourselves, unconditionally. When I give with an open heart, I start a never-ending circle that always comes back to me tenfold. I give a little and get a lot.

June 7

SAYING NO

If I have to say "no" more than once, it's time to discuss the other person's persistence. When others are too pushy and won't accept *no* as an answer, I need to set a boundary without upsetting myself or the other person. Getting upset only hurts me. In the past, I would fall into heated arguments with others over their pushiness and it would escalate to the point where we would no longer speak. I wanted to be better than this and stop losing relationships, so I set out to make some changes. First, I realized others may not be aware of their pushiness so I must have more patience and tolerance. If I am going to open their eyes by declining and diffusing the situation, it must be done in a calm manner. Leading with this approach brings out a better version of others by my example. Then, we both ease into a conversation and lose the argument, not the person.

June 8

SENSITIVITY

Being sensitive to the needs and wants of others is a gift, but
hypersensitivity can be a curse. One of my first clues that I am
being too sensitive is when I interpret the way others speak to me
as judgmental. Perception is everything. How I view and process
conversations with others begins in my mind. And when I'm not in
my right mind, I can misinterpret the meaning behind others' words.
When I'm standing on line at the store and someone politely points
out that I can move up a little, if I'm not thinking straight, I will
hear "MOVE IT LADY!" This is me being overly sensitive, blowing
everything out of proportion. Acting from this flawed perception
can cause harm to others and must be worked on immediately if I
am to be at peace with myself and others. Now, when I feel sensitive,
I try to remember it's my perception that's off, not the other person.
I remain vigilant and pray to see everything as it really is, remaining
as calm as I can until my moment of hypersensitivity passes.
Knowing this about myself has helped me tremendously in all
my relationships.

June 9

BEGINNING, MIDDLE, ENDING

Every event in life has a beginning, a middle, and an ending. My wife brought this to my attention when I was going through a rough patch in my life; this notion helped me get through, putting everything into perspective. When I'm able to break down an event like this, I'm reassured that everything passes and nothing stays the same. No matter how painful or stressful an event may be, I find this to be very comforting. Asking myself where I am on the journey—at the beginning, middle, or end—helps me gauge where I am in the healing process and how much more I must endure to be cured. It fills me with hope and healing, knowing as time progresses the pain will lessen. This idea has huge healing power. During difficult times, remind yourself that there is a beginning, middle, and end to everything, and you will arrive at the end in due course.

June 10

LET THEM FLY

Children are our most valuable treasure in life, a gift from God. Your assignment, if you are a parent, stepparent, guardian, or foster parent, is to be the best caretaker you can while on earth, instilling all the values of goodness you have come to know, protecting them fiercely. You nurture, teach, and inspire them to become the best they can, then leave the rest to God. You can raise them, but you can't run their lives. Watching children grow into adults and making decisions for themselves is scary, and we sometimes worry ourselves sick when they leave the house. But we must let them fly and hope the values we instilled will kick in, leading them to make the right decisions. Even when children move away from your realm of protection, they are never outside God's realm of protection. God is everywhere you can't be and is always watching over them, protecting our precious children, whatever their age, wherever they are. They are God's children and came from God before they left the womb. So, let them fly. God's got them.

June 11

LISTEN TO LEARN

Listening is an art and another form of giving of yourself. Without practicing this important means of communication, our relationships and interactions will surely fail—whether at work, at home, with friends, in business or shopping transactions, everywhere. We all want and need to be heard, and must realize that listening is just as important as talking. But when you're talking, I sometimes find myself thinking about what I'm going to say when it's my turn to talk. This of course is *not* listening. Truly listening to what others have to say takes work and requires paying attention to what is being said, not to what you're going to say next. Every conversation is not always about you and your needs. When you actively listen, it shows you care about what others have to say by being unselfish and giving of yourself. Our conversations become more meaningful with a give-and-take flow between talking and listening. That way, when the conversation ends, both walk away feeling satisfied.

June 12

NO REGRETS, ONLY LOVE

If only I didn't eat so much, my clothes would fit properly. If only I could have saved more money when I was young, I would have a nest egg. If only I would have given more love in past relationships. On and on and on we go and continue to spiral into the shame of regrets, suffocating on our thoughts and becoming more depressed. The longer we hold on to guilt, the sicker we become. At some point we must understand that we can't change the past and must let it go. What's done is done and there is no going back. Holding myself accountable for my past actions is healthy but should only last a short time; then I must let myself off the hook by forgiving myself. God has already forgiven you so now, forgive yourself. Remembering that I did the best I could at those times in my life helps me heal, and I can move forward having no regrets, only love.

June 13

WHAT ARE YOU WAITING FOR?

It doesn't matter how low you have sunk, what you did, who you hurt, or where you are on the spiritual spectrum. God will meet you wherever you are and forgive you so long as you are contrite. I know this firsthand and have been forgiven for many things I've done. All we need is to be sorry for our mistakes, become willing to set things right with others, make direct amends to those we have hurt, and change our behavior so as not to commit the same harmful act. Many of us live with the mistakes of our past and continue to make them, thinking we will never be forgiven. But this is a ploy our egos play on us to keep us held hostage. There is true freedom when we ask for forgiveness. God is waiting for you right now. Since we all have free will, God will only intervene if you ask and He needs your invitation. What are you waiting for?

June 14

MAKE YOURSELF READY

God is omnipresent. Billboards, TV, and radio are all used by God to send messages to those who seek answers to their prayers. God will even use strangers on the street to give you the answer to your prayers if you are open and willing to listen. When you are praying for specific answers, keep an open mind and God will reach you. All you need do is make yourself ready to receive by remaining open. Don't plan or judge where or when the answer may come from, just be open to receive or you will miss it. If you didn't like the looks of the mail carrier, would you turn him away and not let him make his delivery to you? Of course not. It's the same principle. God can and will use anything to deliver our message, but we must always be open and ready and not judge the messenger.

June 15

SUNRISE OF A NEW DAY

When I awaken to a beautiful sunrise, I think, "Thank you God for another day." My heart fills with gratitude that my Creator has given me another day on this planet to try again and get it right. That's what a sunrise means to me. Refresh and renew. Wake up and try again. New thoughts for a new day. I am filled with the hope of new beginnings and a new perspective to begin my day. Whatever my concerns were yesterday, I can start over today and make everything better by applying new understanding and thinking, and realize once again, anything is possible. If God can make a sunrise after darkness, imagine what He can do in you!

June 16

ENDURE TO BE CURED

When life is painful and we are going through tough times, remember that we only have to endure for one minute, one hour, one day at a time. Break time down to the smallest increment to help you get through and keep the faith. Everyone from ancient Sufi poets to our parents have reminded us that "This too shall pass." Your pain will pass and so will your problems. But often the pain must be endured for you to be cured. Emotional turmoil always precedes peace, so use your pain as part of achieving your goal. The solution is on the way. Hold on, keep the faith, endure, and you will be brought to a better place.

June 17

INTERIOR IS THE NEW EXTERIOR

Don't allow the world to define what beauty is for you. For a very long time, I bought into the world's distorted view of the preferred female image of a beautiful body, which holds up young anorexic girls and only their exterior image as the ideal. The media, fashion, and beauty "experts" have set the bar so high and unreachable that it leaves young girls, and even mature women, feeling inadequate. In extreme cases, young girls have killed themselves because they can't achieve this ultrathin image and therefore think they are worthless. The truth is each of us is a unique creation of God and there is no one else on the planet like us. Our size and shape are unique, too. We are like stars in the universe, not one the same as the other. We all have special qualities and abilities and are all different, but together make up a beautiful sky. Start rejecting the foolish standards of an industry so out of touch with God's reality. Be who you are and love yourself, that's the true standard to live by. Make your interior more important than your exterior.

June 18

WHO MOVED?

When you're afraid, feeling alone, and going through a rough patch, remember to look back and see how God got you through other past challenges. Then ask yourself, "Who moved?" You will find God didn't move; your faith did. You were never really alone. God was always with you, right beside you all along. That same God who got you through previous struggles is waiting to help you again; all you need to do is invite God back in. Your willingness is the key that opens the door. Hold on. Recharge your faith and ask God for help. No matter how many times you ask, God will always be there for you once you become willing.

June 19

Hit the Light Switch

Upon awakening each day, I must decide who I am going to be. There are two choices always in front of me—the positive me, who cares about others and does for others, and the negative me, who is selfish and cares only about herself. This is a choice I have to make and remake not only every morning, but throughout the course of every day. Some days, making the right choice doesn't come as naturally as I would like. But the good news is, I know this and am prepared to change from the negative me to the positive me, as many times as it takes. Just as I have faith when I hit the light switch in my home that the lamp will go on, I also have the faith that when I choose and reach for the goodness within me, it will always be there. I'm the one who can flip the switch.

June 20

AS GOD SEES

Can you imagine what it's like seeing through the eyes of God? I imagine God sees us all with love and acceptance, not judgment as some of us were taught. The way I see God depends on how I perceive myself. If I see myself as loving, caring, and tolerant, I will see God as the same. But if I see myself negatively or if I place judgment on others and am angry, then I see an angry God who judges. Our perceptions determine how we come to believe and worship God. We can all have our own idea of God and make it whatever we want. For me, I keep it simple: God is Love. Pure, unconditional love. God does not judge and sees the beauty in each and every one of us. No matter how hard it may seem for us to see this beauty in each other at times, it is still there nonetheless. God sees with the clearest vision, without filters, and I strive each day to make this vision, my vision.

June 21

OFF THE HOOK

Apologizing was never easy for me growing up. Everything was always the other person's fault since I was the master of pointing the finger. To me, an apology meant I lost, that I was a loser. The only time I made an apology was to get myself off the hook from whatever trouble I got myself into, never taking responsibility for my part. Since turning my life around, I have begun to look at myself and see my part in arguments or problems that arise with others. Now, offering an apology means so much more. Once I see my mistake and take responsibility for my actions, an apology is necessary for me to forgive myself and start over. I restore peace to my soul and live happy again without resentment. Today, making an apology is not about the other person, but about my own self-care, getting myself off the hook from my emotions and negative thinking.

June 22

HONOR GOD

Take time to honor God. Spend time in prayer and meditation each day thanking the universe for all your blessings. Prayer and meditation connect us with the almighty power of the universe, filling us with strength and hope. I always start each day with a prayer of thanksgiving for all that God has given me, appreciating every miracle that has been granted to me. A simple prayer of thanksgiving goes a long way and will attract more blessings into your life. When you have a thankful mindset, your wants and needs are satisfied and we are reminded once again that God will always provide for us as long as we trust and have faith. Count your blessings by honoring the one power of the universe that gives life to us all.

June 23

WHERE ARE YOU?

If today were your last day on earth, how would you spend it? Thinking about bills? The fight with your boss? The mix-up with the insurance company? I don't think so. Drop all those thoughts right now, let those worries go, and focus on what's in front of you, right where you are. Rearrange your priorities and state of mind now! Take one thing at a time. Stay in the now. Bills will be paid. Problems will be solved. Maybe not today, but eventually. Walking around with these things in the forefront of your mind will drive you crazy, and you will miss the opportunities God is sending you right now because your mind is elsewhere. I practice staying right where I am by asking myself, "Where are you?" throughout the day, to keep my mind from wandering away from the only thing I can control, which is the present moment.

June 24

DON'T JUMP

Are you at a crossroad, struggling with a decision? Hold on. Don't jump into or off anything. Many times, I didn't know which way to turn and needed the guidance of others. In times like this, it's best to take a breath and say a prayer, asking God to guide you. When I ask through prayer for God to show me the way, I am directed in my decision-making or challenges I am facing. Then, I can consult with another person, a trusted wise friend, or even a professional in the mental health field. My answers come and I receive the guidance I need to be restored to peace. God speaks through people, so look for your message to come through others. And, don't jump! When you need help, call someone.

June 25

NO CROWDING

Being emotionally dependent on others is harmful and draining to both people. By doing this, you make the other person God, which will breed more insecurity and resentment when they cannot fulfill the demands being made on them. At some point in life, we all need to grow up and become responsible for ourselves, stand on our own two feet, and not continue to burden others. Letting go can be very scary but that's when we grow. We need to create a space between ourselves and others so God may enter. God can only enter into equal partnerships and cannot come in when we have crowded ourselves too close to another. When we create space for God, our spirit and self-esteem expand, and we allow ourselves the ability to stand alone and become independent with a healthy dependence on God.

June 26

FINISH!

Don't go halfway. Go all the way. Nothing good comes from half measures. Imagination and perspiration are good for the body, mind, and spirit. They lead to inspiration, which is vital to accomplishing your goals. When body, mind, and spirit are all three working together, they form a trinity, which is necessary to succeed in anything worthwhile. So, dive in. If you never finish anything, you'll never know you can. Start with simple things. Make an aim to begin something you always wanted to do today. Then, finish what you set out to do, even if it's just step one. Who knows where it will lead? See things through and don't quit; miracles and opportunities often arrive at the eleventh hour. Accomplishing something important takes a lot of hard work and diligence, and consistency is the key to completion and success. But first, finish!

June 27

HOLD ON

Waiting for outcomes can be long and tedious, not as easy or comfortable as we would like. I pray, nothing happens, and I feel like quitting and giving up. In times like these, hold on. Changes are about to take place that are the best we could ever hope for. We don't see the changes happening because God works on the unseen plane, and that takes time. Many times, I have quit before my miracle came and lost valuable lessons life had to teach me. But no more. Now when I have to wait on outcomes in my life, I know that as I am waiting, my faith is being tested while my trust and relationship with God is growing stronger. My part is to pray and let it go, while I let God deliver me to what's best for me. Another dividend from waiting is I learn patience and understand that my miracle may be right behind my desire to give up.

June 28

HAVE YOU FORGIVEN ME YET?

Are you waiting for someone to forgive you for harms you have caused? If you are, you need to listen right now. Receiving forgiveness from others is not required. Forgiving ourselves is mandatory. If I had to wait for others to forgive me for my past mistakes, I would still be an emotional basket case full of remorse and guilt. I had to learn how to forgive myself for what I have done to others. It took time and lots of prayer, but I learned that forgiving oneself comes as a natural result of forgiving others. When I began to look over my life at the mistakes I made, I went out and started making my amends and forgiving others. By doing so, the guilt and remorse I was feeling was lifted from me by God. When you forgive yourself, you are in turn forgiven. This paradox changes my life when I practice it.

June 29

SPIRITUAL CLEANSE

Modern science suggests that there is a direct link between negative thoughts stored in the body and physical illness. In my own experience, it took me some time but now I see the correlation. I was always running to the doctor all the time saying, "I'm sick," trying to treat from the outside in with medication. But when I began resolving my mental and emotional health internally, my symptoms and so-called sicknesses dissipated. I believe that most of my physical ailments stemmed from past hurts I was holding onto, like resentment, guilt, and shame. I needed to purge these toxic emotions if I was to ever to be healthy. I needed a spiritual cleansing. Taking an honest look at my assets and liabilities, using prayer, forgiving others, and most importantly, learning to let go of debilitating thought patterns, has changed my life miraculously. God entered my life and rearranged the furniture. The more spiritually, emotionally, and mentally healthy I became, the more I noticed my physical body following suit. Cleansing myself through the grace of God spiritually and mentally has led me to find true peace, happiness, and health.

June 30

UNLEASH LOVE

There is a simple solution to life's problems, which we all carry with us, that can right the wrongs and costs nothing. Whatever we are going through, the power of love will heal it. Love is the answer, so what's the question? Quarreling with family members? Unleash love. Can't get along with co-workers? Unleash love. Give love in all situations, no matter what, and hold love as the focal point of your life. Many times, we hold back love for fear of rejection. But that is loving with conditions. The universe will respond when we love unconditionally, and God will heal any situation into which we unleash love. Wherever you may be on the path or whatever your current circumstances, reset and recharge your life by giving love, and love will likewise enter. God will replace, restore, and realign our lives for good more abundantly than we could ever imagine when we put love first.

July 1

FREE WILL

One of the greatest freedoms we are blessed to have is free will. Our free will allows us to explore and become whatever we want. It is our birthright; we were created with it. It gives us the power to choose between right and wrong, who to pray and worship to, who we want to love, how we want to dress, where we want to live, ad infinitum. If it weren't for this precious freedom of choice, we would all be robots meandering around the planet. How boring! Having free will gives us the right to choose what's best for us. For example, it allows me to choose to live with a God in my life, or without. Again, it's my choice and a great comfort to me knowing I'm never forced or coerced into believing in anything I'm not comfortable with. Through many failures in my life, I had to find something other than myself to believe in, and thankfully, I have found a God of my understanding that is always ready to help me, if I ask. But, because of free will, I have to seek. God shows up through invitation only. I must use my free will and ask for assistance through the power of prayer and only then will God intercede on my behalf. God will never intrude or impede on the choices we make. Such is the power of free will, this blessed gift of freedom.

July 2

BAD DAY OR BAD MOMENT?

Even when we are only having a bad moment, we usually say we're
having a bad day. We tend to sit in our stuff longer than we should,
much like a child sitting in a dirty diaper. We become overly fixated
on the problem, sinking deeper into the abyss of negative thinking,
until our obsessed thinking derails us. You are just a thought away
from turning it all around. NOW. You can begin again. Why wait?
What good is waiting going to do, when you will eventually need to
work through the bad moment anyway? You can control how a bad
moment affects you and how long you choose to suffer by changing
your thinking. The way out is to accept the current situation exactly
the way it is and let it go. Chalk it up to one bad moment, and
then focus on the solution. To turn your bad day into a bad
moment, get your mind going in a different direction, which
will lead to a good day.

July 3

OWN IT

A truth is not "owned" until it is incorporated into your being and change occurs. This is a process. I can say the words "I forgive you," but until I actually stop taking swipes at you and see my part in the offense, they are empty words and I have not "owned" the truth. Seeing past the hurt to the goodness in the offender is necessary before we can truly heal and forgive. This takes time and prayer. When my thinking and behavior change as a result of thoughtful reflection and prayer, then I "own" my statement of forgiveness. That ability is there in all of us. We find it by working on owning our truths, knowing we are not perfect, and releasing others for their mistakes. God in turn releases us through forgiveness.

July 4

LET GO OR GET DRAGGED

Acceptance doesn't have to come after breaking your head against a wall. You can reach for acceptance just as you reach for your morning cup of coffee. All you need do is make the decision to accept the situation you cannot control and let go. Life can be difficult, but letting go brings much peace. Think of this visual: you are holding onto a rope that is connected to a fast-moving car. The car continues to drive faster and you hold on tighter, eventually falling to the pavement at high speed. Now you're a bloodied mess and you realize you could have let go sooner, when the car was moving slowly. Yet this is what we often do in life. We hold on to a hopeless situation, a doomed relationship, a dead-end job, and get dragged instead. So, which is it for you? Let go or get dragged? Now letting go seems like a simple decision.

July 5

YOUR GREATNESS AWAITS

Go after what makes you happy. Stop wasting time wondering if you're good enough because you are. Plug into your God-given drive and determination and that will aid you in your quest for greatness. Go for it. Make the move that's on your mind today and remember the life you want is waiting for you, a thought away. Don't stay stuck and frustrated. Ask God to help you through prayer to make your dreams a reality. Why waste precious time instead of acting? Only you can make the decision to change your life today. Do it now. Your greatness awaits. You deserve all the happiness of your dreams.

July 6

EVERYONE ELSE IS TAKEN

Oscar Wilde once advised, "Be yourself. Everyone else is already taken." Are you conforming to what the world thinks you should be even if that doesn't fit the person you are or aspire to be? Denying who you are is living a lie and you will never find happiness that way, no matter how much you deny yourself or try to rationalize your behavior. Be proud of who you are right now and step into your truth. This is your birthright. We are perfect creations in God's eyes, made from love to be happy, joyous, and free. Express your inner beauty and love yourself. This is living God's will. Come out of your shell and be at peace with yourself, others, and most of all, God. God loves you no matter who you want to love or how you dress. Accept yourself for exactly who you are, loving and living the way that is true to yourself. You will experience true freedom of your spirit and be introduced to the magnificent, loving child of God you are.

July 7

LIVE OUT LOUD

Honesty sets me apart in all my affairs. At work, at home, in all
my relationships, everything is easier with honesty leading the way.
Lying or evading the truth starts drama, invites distrust, and weakens
relationships. In the end, lies become very difficult to keep up with
and will only hurt *you* and nothing good comes from that. Living
a lie is a trap. Sometimes it seems lying may be the easier way, but
the truth always surfaces. However difficult my life is today, I am
honest with myself and others so I can live free from drama and all
that goes with it. I put my life under a looking glass and am truthful
in all things, living out loud. Without pretense, and with no hidden
agenda, I am honest with all people. This creates an environment for
others to feel safe around me so they can be honest too.

July 8

TAKE YOUR PILL

Sometimes, we all go through sadness and unhappiness, which can cause depression by stewing in our problems for way too long. Thinking only of myself and my own problems causes negative thoughts to swallow up my happiness. I once descended into a dark hole and felt I couldn't come out of it. When those dark thoughts linger, as mine did, it may cross over into clinical depression. When this happened to me, at first I chose to self-medicate. Then, the time came when those substances didn't work anymore and I had to find another solution. Working with professionals has helped me get to the root causes of my unhappiness, face my demons, and work on the underlying issues that have kept me in isolation. I no longer need to take any medication and now see that until your mind changes, your life cannot change. Finding and focusing only on the goodness in my life and having gratitude for all I have are the two most important things necessary in living a happy life without undue sadness or crippling depression. Now, each day I take a "gratitude pill" with only good side effects.

July 9

IF IT IS BROKE, DON'T FIX IT

Give up! Put your arms in the air today and surrender. Stop banging your head against the wall and move on. Some relationships were not meant to be. We keep at it in the hopes things will change. But they never do, and you are constantly battling to save something that is broken and can't be fixed. It's okay to walk away. Sometimes, even if it *is* broke, don't fix it. However, do remember to keep good thoughts about the other person and wish them well. When we leave any relationship, it's always best to let it be on good terms or we will take any residual negative energy with us to the next relationship. Just know you tried your best. Then move on.

July 10

INSTANT GRATIFICATION

When I want a quick shot of instant gratification, I no longer look to drink or drug to get it. Now I go out and help someone. I give of myself—my time, my money, or I lend an ear. This lifts my spirit EVERY time, taking me out of myself to a place called happiness. When I help others, I instantly forget all my cares and concerns and I realize once again how good my life really is. Too much focus on ourselves and our problems only leads to depression and self-centeredness. Each day I make an effort to do something for another person and not tell anyone. I keep it between me and God and am always rewarded for my good deeds in some way. Make it a practice in your life too for it will keep you and your problems in check and give you that peaceful existence we all crave. It's the best kind of instant gratification.

July 11

LET THEM SKIN THEIR KNEES

Parenting has to be the hardest job on the planet! God has entrusted you with a human being whom you are responsible to teach and nurture on His behalf. That's a huge responsibility. Parents must be up to the challenge and perform 365 days a year, for the rest of their lives. One of the toughest lessons a parent has to go through is letting children "skin their knees." By letting go, they teach their children how to become responsible and independent, making their own decisions. If not, parents run the risk of the child becoming emotionally dependent on them and never growing into a responsible adult. As parents, the hard part is watching them make mistakes but remembering mistakes are part of learning and growing. Instruct them as best you can and leave the rest to them and God. God will prepare a way for them and protect them. These valuable lessons learned by both parent and child are part of God's plan and helps each grow in faith.

July 12

THOUGHT HOARDER

Stop putting things off. Do what you need to do. Take care of chores and necessary tasks when they are first on your radar. Often, we miss important opportunities the universe is sending us because we are still stuck on what should have been dealt with beforehand. In the physical world, undone tasks pile up, create clutter, and cause a mess. There is also an emotional cost that weighs us down when we don't let things go. The more we don't attend to what needs to be done, the more we mentally give up too. That mental laziness stops us from achieving our greatest potential. We procrastinate and become *thought hoarders*. Just as creating clutter in your home makes you a hoarder, procrastination is clutter of the mind and makes you a thought hoarder. Make way for clear thinking by cleaning up your thoughts.

July 13

WHO IS DRIVING?

Would falling asleep at the wheel while driving be okay? No, of course not. It might be instant death. The same applies to our thoughts. Stay awake to what you are thinking about and don't fall asleep mentally. That's when mayhem enters, and we are no longer actively driving the car of our own life. Trying to navigate through life while mentally asleep can be a disaster; you never know where that ride will end up—crashing and burning most likely. Each day give your thoughts over to God and your ride will be smooth. You may hit some rough patches but know reaching your destination will always be safe.

July 14

SWIM ON

Facing the trauma of witnessing my grandmother and mother take their final breaths is something I work on each day. I was there when both died, and the experiences changed me forever. Wanting to escape the pain of these tragedies from constantly playing in my mind is one of the most difficult things I have ever had to go through. Some days, the grief was so big it would swallow me up; but today, thankfully, I know differently. The pain comes but the pain also leaves. Getting to the other side of grief is still a daily process for me, but now I have tools to help me get my mind back to a safe place. Using prayer and changing my thoughts is how I survive. Reminding myself that both of my loved ones are in a better place watching over me is my mantra on the difficult days. Coping with grief is like being in the ocean swimming toward the shore. Some days the shore is close and I make it to dry land, unscathed, and other days it seems so distant, I feel as if I'm going to drown. But, on those days, I swim on in spite of where I am knowing I will get back to shore safely.

July 15

SAY IT!

In our relationships with others, when something needs to be said, say it. This is true communication and the only way to get to a resolution. Walking around on eggshells does not resolve anything. We rationalize our own fear of confronting others by telling ourselves, *I'm too angry to talk and it will come out wrong.* When the truth needs to be told to others, don't be afraid to speak up. Say it. If your words come out wrong, you can always go back and apologize for the way you presented it. We strive for self-restraint, but getting the message across to someone who really needs to hear what you have to say is what's most important. The truth needs to be told and the sin in these cases is withholding the truth, not in how it might be delivered. The other person may even thank you later for waking them up from their slumber.

July 16

A Drug Is a Drug Is a Drug

What is calling you to do damage today? Food, drugs, alcohol, anxiety, fear? A drug is a drug is a drug. They will all keep you in bondage and kill you if left unchecked. Whatever it is, you don't have to listen. There is another way to live if you just reach out for help. There are many people in the world who suffer from the same issues as you and they are living happy, healthy lives now because at some point in the past they chose to call out for help. I am one of them and have come through to the other side. You are not unique, nor are your problems. Your story has been told before by countless others who have come up and out of the abyss by reaching out for help. You're not going to die by asking for help. You may die if you don't. There are people waiting for you to show up so they can confide how they are no longer living a life of misery because they asked for help and didn't die. Our lives have been saved to help others get better. There are many options available to all who suffer. I've come to see that suffering is a choice, and we can make a different choice each day if we seek help. Whatever the drug is, seek help and find out how to put that drug down.

July 17

EMOTIONAL HANGOVERS

Ever have an emotional hangover? You probably did but never called it that. Much like the feeling you get after a night of too many drinks, an emotional hangover can come from experiencing an emotionally trying time, or after you've indulged in wallowing in your emotions. Arguing with others, anxiety, or being afraid can trigger powerful emotions that take their toll on you. The next day, you're emotionally spent, physically tired, perhaps nasty to people, and your body may even feel weak. These are the symptoms of an emotional hangover and they can last for days depending on the situation. So, know this: there is a price we pay when we indulge too long in coddling our negative emotions. You're guaranteed an emotional hangover. Try to acknowledge your emotions when they first come up and work on them immediately, instead of letting them fester until you are overloaded. This helps avoid the traps that lead to emotional hangovers.

July 18

WILL YOU ANSWER?

Change happens for a reason and for some of us, the reason is that standing still is simply no longer an option. We're forced to make a move. Perhaps we have outgrown our current job, or the life we once knew no longer serves our highest good. We've stopped growing because God has other plans for us. Like a caterpillar turning into a beautiful butterfly, we also occasionally must change and grow into the new being our soul yearns to become. Evolving spiritually is our birthright and can happen when we're aware of it, or sometimes subconsciously. Either way when it's time to wake up to our full potential and fulfill our destiny here, you will be led to your natural place in this world. Many in life are called. Will you answer?

July 19

OPPORTUNITIES

Opportunities come and go in our lives. The wise person prays for fruitful opportunities and waits for them to arrive while others watch them pass by like a parade while complaining the world has nothing to offer them. Pray and wait for your opportunities. And when they arrive, be alert and recognize them. Grab them and run with them. When God opens a window, don't pull down the shade. Your next opportunity may be the very thing you have waited for your whole life—even though it may not seem like that at first. So never judge the opportunity; be objective and try it. Sometimes opportunities come disguised as something other than what you expected. Be open and let God guide you. If it's meant to be, the journey will be effortless. That's how you know your opportunity has arrived.

July 20

BE SWITZERLAND

When a situation doesn't concern you, stay neutral and let others work things out. If not, you are meddling and taking sides; others may be hurt and feel as if your involvement amounts to ganging up on them. Stepping in and taking sides shows favoritism, creates dissension, and is divisive, which is hurtful and drives people away. Better to restrain yourself to be objective, and back off. Let others invite you into the fray if they need your help. The world doesn't need any more buttinskies. Sticking your nose into other people's problems or business without being asked ultimately will alienate you from others and can cause irreparable harm to all parties. Be Switzerland. Switzerland is a neutral country, never taking sides in armed conflicts between other nations. We can all learn a lot from their example. Show others you care about both sides and will always help them find common ground *if* they want assistance.

July 21

HOST OR HOSTAGE?

Are you a host to God or a hostage to your ego? Don't answer until you give it some thought. Being a host to God includes giving freely without expecting anything in return. Unconditional loving. Period. No strings attached. Being a hostage to your ego is the opposite: giving with expectations and strings always attached, a form of control and manipulation that will lead to destruction in your relationships. You will either be a hostage or take a hostage with this mentality. When we are a host to God, we let others be who they are without judgment, without trying to change them. With that attitude, we form true friendships and bonds that last a lifetime. Live and let live and be a host to God.

July 22

ARE YOU A GOOD TIMEKEEPER?

Making the most of time, in time, after some time, time to go, time to stay—we talk about time a lot. Time *is* important. But are you a good timekeeper? Does time master you or are you a master of your time? Do you let time take you hostage? Running to beat the clock, cramming too much into too little time, and losing track of time all serve no purpose but to keep you off balance by creating chaos and, as a result, unwise decisions. Make your time work *for* you. Plan each day wisely. Carve out enough time to complete what you can successfully accomplish with ease and no more. There will be more time for the rest tomorrow. It's that simple. Organize and discipline yourself to become a good timekeeper and you will get more done than ever before.

July 23

SAY "THANK YOU"

Thank you are the two most underrated words in our language. Saying them to others will bring feelings of gratitude and love and connect us to each other spiritually. Say "thank you" whenever you can—to the clerk at the store, to your family members, your friends, the mail carrier. The underlying respect and appreciation expressed by those two words are much needed in today's world and everyone deserves to hear them. Teach the importance of these words in your own home, where all true values are born and modeled. Passing on this powerful expression of love is our duty and what God expects of us. Mamas and Papas, please raise your children with "Thank you." The world will thank you back.

July 24

WIGGLEBUTT

If you are lucky enough to have a dog, you are blessed with such unconditional love. For me, there is nothing better than coming home after a rough day and being greeted by my howling wigglebutt! Yes, wigglebutt! That uncontrolled movement dogs make with their behind, letting you know they are just as happy to see you as you are of them! And waking up to her furry face on my pillow is a joy unlike anything I've ever felt before and is something I look forward to every morning. It makes me smile and my heart feels like it will explode with love looking into her eyes. What a great way to start the day! My dog Mollie is a rescue and she rescues me every day. Pets save us from ourselves, not the other way around. They teach us unconditional love in the face of everything and keep us happy, getting us through the tough times. Our lives become fulfilled and enriched with a love and bond we share that stems deep within our souls; a connection beyond this world to some other place, a knowing we were together before. All of my beautiful dogs I've raised over the years were a godsend and a blessing to me. Each one of them had a purpose in my life and got me through some difficult times. I will always be grateful to all my wigglebutts for their love.

July 25

BLESSINGS

Blessings come in many forms and guises. I have experienced many in my own life. You never know when they will show up. My biggest blessings were finding ways to change my thinking and behaviors. These blessings led to a new life for me on many levels: I no longer am addicted to drugs or alcohol, smoke cigarettes, or hide who I am. Now I pray for God to let me use my experiences as a blessing to the world, through my writings, telling my story of hope to help heal others. I receive my own blessings when I share my experiences with all who want and need to hear them, spreading hope in our sometimes hopeless world—and in turn, that is a blessing to others.

July 26

THE MAGIC LANE

Having faith through difficult circumstances wakes up something very special in us and the universe. This is the when miracles arrive and when they do, it's as if heaven opens a magic lane within you that you never knew existed. When the magic lane appears, it invites you to make a complete turnaround of your life by giving you strength not ordinarily your own. You are now able to do, feel, think, and act as never before. Suddenly, your thinking is directed above the problem onto the solution and your previous, negative thought system has changed with a new, positive one taking its place. We are rewired and reborn. Your life as you once knew it will be forever changed when the magic lane appears.

July 27

THE COMMITTEE IS IN SESSION

A ping pong game is often underway in my head. *Should I or shouldn't I? Take the job, not take the job? Go on a diet, not diet? Eat the cake, don't eat the cake?* When this happens, my head is full with an endless round of indecision and I want to take it off my body and place it on the table for a rest. My mind continually races with conflicting thoughts. When this happens, I tell myself that while the "committee is in session," I need a break. Too many voices are speaking and I need someone to consider them all and then overrule some. Time to quiet my mind. So, I pray, and prayer always helps me get back to my center of being, puts God back in charge, and quiets the committee so I can sort out my best decision.

July 28

GRIEVING AND ACCEPTANCE

Grieving a loved one who has passed is an unfortunate part of life that we all must go through. There are no rules for grief. Everyone has their own way of processing the pain. The hardest part of grief includes the acceptance that I will never see someone again in this life. Letting them go and accepting this is something I work on daily and will likely be with me my whole life. I have experienced a lot of loss and whether it's a family member, a beloved pet, or a friend, the pain is the same. At times, the hurt was so painful, it has taken my breath away and left me feeling paralyzed. Above me was a dark cloud that I could not shake and beneath me was a dark hole. I've come to know from others who have experienced this that I am not alone in what I feel. The intense emotions we experience while grieving are similar, and acceptance is something we must each come to in our own way and time. When grief wells up in me now, I want it out of my body and my tears are the way it escapes. I let myself cry when I need to, never holding it in for this will only delay my healing. I talk about my departed loved ones and talk *to them*. This all brings me closer to the acceptance I need to heal, knowing their spirits live on and I will see them all again one sweet day.

July 29

DISCIPLINE

Without the precious practice of discipline, I can never achieve my goals. I can pray until I'm purple, but if I'm not consistent in my efforts and actions, all will be lost. A prayer here and there, paying lip service to God, will not bring me to my desired goal. Staying focused and disciplined, putting in the work, taking actions, and praying to God for the strength while setting out to do whatever necessary— that's what delivers success. When I'm serious about my goals and not being wishy-washy, the universe responds and unleashes the power I need to bring me the changes I am working for. When I am disciplined and get serious with the universe, the universe gets serious with me.

July 30

The Race Mind

Ever experience the race mind? Some call it an anxiety attack. Whatever you choose to call it, the effects are the same. Your thoughts are racing out of control, flooding your mind with everything you should and should not be doing, making you feel overwhelmed and you can't stop it. You begin to drown on your own thoughts. It's as if you drank 12 cups of coffee in succession and are suffocating in your own thoughts. Sound familiar? We all get overwhelmed in life and need a remedy for this. Some take medication to relieve their anxiety and others use prayer and meditation. I tried both but when I started using prayer and meditation, it healed me and has no side effects except peace. Practicing prayer and meditation has a calming effect on slowing me down and bringing balance back into my life, keeping anxiety away. Overdoing, overworking, becoming overemotional, and doing too much of anything, tips the scales of balance in my life, which brings on anxiety and the race mind. It is then I'm reminded I cannot do it all and need to slow down and do one thing at a time to bring me back to sanity.

July 31

GATHER YOUR CHEERLEADERS

Who do you want by your side when things go wrong in life? I gather my cheerleaders. Having the support and love of others is a blessing and something I cherish. Life, and the lessons it brings, can be difficult at times and having family and friends rally around me when I need their support has helped me get through many tough times. They are my cheerleaders and I hold them very close to my heart. They hold me up, give me a shoulder to cry on, and love and protect me fiercely until I can love myself again. Their gentleness brings me back from the dead and lightens my burdens with the ease of their voices and their very presence. I can't imagine life without my cheerleaders or where I would be today without their unselfish acts of true compassion and empathy. My cheerleaders are gifts from God.

August 1

DON'T CRAM, SCRAM

Slow down. The universe wasn't built in a day. Most projects fail because we try to do too much all at once. Let things unfold, one day at time. Pray for guidance each day and God will lead you to what's next. The most thoughtful plans are the ones that succeed because they cover all the angles, without any surprises. Preparing yourself daily with just enough work for this day will lead you to success. Cramming 10 days of work into one week will only lead to disaster. When you are of this mindset, your work becomes harder and you will sabotage your progress. That's when it's time to scram. Yes, get up and walk away for a time. When you return, you will have a fresher perspective and your creative juices can reorganize. By slowing down and inserting breaks in your day, you can enjoy what you're doing. Break down your projects into increments of only what you can successfully do in one day. Without cramming, everything will get done with ease.

August 2

I'm Grateful To...

Each day, we all have a list of things to do in our daily lives. Some items we enjoy, others not so much. But if you think about it, how blessed are we to have these chores that support the comfortable lives we live? Instead of viewing our daily routine as a grind, forgetting how truly blessed we are, we need to remember how lucky we are. When it's rainy and cold outside, I might say, "I have to walk my dog," with some disdain behind it, forgetting how much joy and love I feel for my pet and how much I appreciate her. Or, waking up some days saying, "I have to go to work," forgetting how blessed I am to have a job in the changing times we live in. We take a lot for granted and it could all be gone in a second. Turn it around and remember how blessed you are by replacing "I have to..." with "I'm grateful to..." This reframing will remind you to appreciate what you have and put gratitude front and center.

August 3

A Prayer of Thanksgiving

Thank you, God, for all that I was, all that I am, and all that I am becoming. This is a great way to start the day, every day. Giving thanks to God for all you have been through ignites true appreciation within. This powerful prayer of thanksgiving will produce an attitude of gratitude that will get your day moving in the ideal direction. And, your attitude will be infectious and bring out the best in other people. When I live in this grateful state of mind, I attract the same goodness from others and am surrounded by love and peace. It's a fact that positive people are more successful in everything they do, especially when they have an attitude of gratitude. Try starting your day with this prayer for a week, faithfully, and see the changes that will bring success and happiness into your life.

August 4

JOY

Joy is such a small word. But such huge feeling is attached to it! For me, joy is a feeling of both peace and contentment, combined with love. When I'm joyful, I emit an invisible signal to the universe that I'm open to miracles and all goods things. God pours love and peace into joyful people who want to bring happiness and peace to the world. There is not enough joy in the world now. We can each help bring joy back by first claiming it for ourselves, then spreading it among others. Claim your joy and spread it to your tribe. Then watch how it creates a ripple effect. That's how we start to change the world, one joyful person at a time.

August 5

MAKE LOVE MATTER

Today, put down your anger, make amends, and forgive others. Whatever was done to you, real or imagined, can be forgiven if you choose to live in peace. Think about this for a minute: If Jesus Christ could forgive those who crucified Him, why can't you forgive others? Besides, you have made mistakes in life and received forgiveness from others, so why deny forgiveness to another? The longer you withhold forgiveness will just prolong your anxiety, the blissful peace, and true freedom that awaits you. Make love matter, nothing else. Be kind to one another. It's a simple act that we can all do. If we all respect each other and share love, we are doing God's will and will always find happiness. We are all children of a loving God and come in all shapes, colors, and genders. God made us all different so we don't get bored—not to judge and hate on each other's differences. Let's put down our prejudice, forgive, find common ground we can all walk together on, and unite as one through the power of love. We owe it to ourselves and generations to come. Make love matter.

August 6

TALK IT OUT

Disagreements between people can be fixed with a simple solution—communication. If we could just discuss issues calmly and respectfully when things go wrong, we can accomplish so much more in our lives and save a lot of unnecessary drama. When we are at odds with another person, we often walk away with resentment and feed ourselves a thousand reasons why we should never speak to the person again. But who do we hurt? The other person doesn't feel a thing. Our resentments hurt only ourselves because when we are angry, we carry negative, toxic emotions inside that will cause us stress and make us miserable. When there is a communication breakdown, instead of tucking away a resentment, use your God-given communication skills and talk it out. Find common ground, have a fruitful conversation, and work from there. Stop burning bridges and instead build new ones you can both cross, leading back to love.

August 7

LOVE IS...

Love is an energy we emit that attracts more love. More love attracts happiness and contentment. In an instant, we can make the choice to love. Doing so will change our day, week, month, year, and lifetime—one day at a time. That's all it takes. Step by step we can rebuild our lives back to being happy, by choosing love. I have made the decision many times in my life to choose love over hate, love over pettiness, love instead of trivial upset—and it has changed my life. When I am in this love mindset, all good things come to me and I attract the people I need. Love-centered minds think alike! We attract what we are. Make love your focus and start attracting everything necessary to change your life.

August 8

REAL LOVE MAKES NO DEMANDS

Some say jealousy shows that a romantic partner really loves you. I say jealousy stems from insecurity and makes a demand on us to keep proving our love. Jealousy is a negative emotion with strings attached, which could never be connected to real love. Real love makes no demands. Jealous acts are a form of control over people, crippling if allowed to continue. The antidote to jealousy is trusting your partner, which originates from trusting in God. We invite God into our relationships so we can keep them in right working order. Love God first, then ourselves, then we can love others. When you have God first in your love relationship, there is no room for demanding jealousy, and trust will come naturally. That is real security that no one can come between.

August 9

ANGELS OF MERCY

I believe that one way God shows us mercy is by sending angels to ease our pain. They hold us up when we go through horrific events that are almost too much to bear; they are here and all around us. I have experienced these beings of light in some of my darkest hours. One thing is for sure, your belief in angels is irrelevant. They will arrive just when you need them, whether you believe or not. Don't think for one minute it is you acting alone when life throws tough challenges your way. None of us are that strong. I continue to witness God's mercy in my life and in the lives of others—in the form of angels. When my mom passed, God's angels of mercy were with her to alleviate her pain and fear. God showed her mercy for all the times she gave it in her life. Mercy comes to us as we show it to others. As the Beatitudes tell us, "Blessed are the merciful, for they shall obtain mercy."

August 10

GOD'S GOT YOU

Losing a job can be catastrophic for some people. I have been there, and it was scary. Worry jumps right to the forefront. How will I pay my mortgage? What about healthcare? All the things we need to survive are questioned. When I lost my business, I didn't know what or where to go and had to rely on the only thing I had left—God. I put all my trust and faith into God. I prayed for a miracle each day, but also moved my feet, looking for jobs. Then finally one day, a new position arrived. And, it was better than any other job I ever had! If you ever find yourself in this spot, do the work to find a new job, but also try faith and pray for a miracle. God's got you. God is bigger than layoffs, and losing your job may be the best thing that ever happens to you by giving you a new life. It may just be the push you needed to get your life going in a different direction you never would have considered on your own. God's got you. Believe it. What you believe manifests in your life.

August 11

WHAT'S YOUR OPINION

We all have opinions and sharing them with others makes great conversation. It's helpful to get everyone's input and different outlooks on events in our lives. Though we may not always agree, we respect each other. But when we find ourselves pushing our opinions on others, often without being invited, or dominating the conversation as we try to convince everyone that our opinion is the right one, that's where trouble begins. When you find yourself doing this, it's time to step back. Having respect for others' opinions and allowing others to share them is how we progress as a society and individually; it's the core of civil discourse. We can all see things differently and still get along. That's the goal. God speaks though us all and we need to hear what everyone has to say. We then have the option to silently dismiss the opinions that aren't helpful or useful.

August 12

JUST FLOAT

Don't push too hard today for what you want. Trying too hard will get you nowhere but tense and anxious. Give your requests to God through prayer and then just let it all go. *Let* is a small word with a big meaning. Let go and let God. Let the master do for you what you cannot do for yourself. God's plan will be so much better than whatever we can devise in our finite minds, while God's infinite guidance will show us the way. I use this simple meditation to help me let go and let God: Sit quietly somewhere where you can be alone without interruption. Now visualize stepping into a boat and floating down the lazy river. Sit back and relax, noticing the beauty of the river and listening as the water laps against your boat. See God as your captain, navigating you through the waters and just float. Be in the moment and enjoy your ride. Your destination will eventually come into view and you will see it with a totally different perspective. Just float.

August 13

NOT JUST ANOTHER DAY

When all your effort and hard work come to fruition, it's not just another routine day. These times are sacred and should be savored like a delicious meal. We remember to take time to give thanks to our Creator for the gifts that have arrived as a result of keeping our faith. We say thank you to God through simple reflection on where we were versus where we are now, plus a deep appreciation for all that is. This step is very important in keeping what we have been given. Only by having a spirit of gratefulness, do we keep what we have. When we achieve a milestone, it's part of a wonderful new life that we may have never known but for the grace of God. Be thankful, be grateful, and remember, it's not just another day.

August 14

HUMAN BEING OR HUMAN DOING?

Stop merely doing things and get back to being. When you are constantly doing, you lose the rhythm of life; you become a robot, getting things done, but not connecting with your spirit and humanity. Even when we don't have a task to complete, we often fill our time, creating busy-ness, being a "human doing." Instead, welcome the slowdown to your fast-paced life. You are an evolving being and may need a short break. The universe knows this. When our lives seem "on hold" it may be a gift we get from God to relax and just be—a human being, not a human doing. Reflect on all you have accomplished in your life with God's guidance and reconnect with the goodness within.

August 15

HAVE YOU AN OPEN MIND?

An open mind is a healthy mind that observes everything without judgment or prejudice, has no agenda to push, and does not try to control outcomes. An open mind sits and watches thoughts like a parade passing by and when it sees something of interest, waits for the right moment, inserts itself, and starts marching. Getting into this state of open-mindedness requires giving up a thought system that perhaps seemed to be working most of your life and was very comfortable. It is a choice we can make each day to create a new way of thinking, which will point our lives in a new direction, opening us up to new opportunities to change and grow as God would have us. Openminded-ness peels away the layers of thinking that no longer serve our highest good and brings new experiences that connect us with others and challenge us to become more of who we really are.

August 16

GOD IS LOVE

I was raised to believe in a punishing God, and even far into adulthood, I thought for sure God would banish me to hell for some of things I had done in my life. So, when I needed help, seeking God did not seem like an option. My solution was to stay as far away from this taskmaster in the sky as possible and make myself God. I created a God in MY image and likeness, portraying fear as the God of my understanding. But when my knees hit the floor and I was out of answers and could not handle my life anymore, my thinking about this God had to be smashed. So, I asked myself, "Why not create a loving God?" When I first started my search for faith, keeping it as simple as "God is love" was about all I could fathom. I related God with love and hoped it was true. Despite my misgivings, I needed something tangible that I could grasp. I began to see God working in my life, healing me and others, through love and compassion. This was the new beginning I waited for my whole life. Now my understanding of God has grown and deepened with love as the foundation, and as my faith grows, many more aspects of God are revealed to me. I found a new strength and faith in a power that is loving, forgiving, and all inclusive. Plus, what a relief to know it's not me!

August 17

FRIEND OR FRIENDLY?

Are you a true friend to others or just friendly? There is an ocean between the two. I've seen the difference in my life. I have true friends for whom I would show up in a minute if needed and other people with whom I am just friendly. We need both kinds of friendship, but having true friends is lifesaving. I have found that the key to having true friends is this: I have to be a friend to others first. Showing respect, kindness, and honesty right from the get-go prepares the way for trust in all my relationships. Putting these attributes forth initially, without waiting for the other person to do it first, is essential in building real friendship. Then the relationship will take on a life of its own, with give and take from both parties. If at some point this stops happening and one person is giving all the time and not getting anything back, it's time to reevaluate and communicate. If not, we risk sliding from true friends to just friendly.

August 18

YOUR SPIRITUAL ZONE

Performing too many things at once can make you crazy. When you find yourself stressing and pushing to get things done, you're not in your spiritual zone. Our multitasking skills are used against us by our egos to convince us that we can do the undoable, and we take on way more than we can handle. Watch out for this pitfall. When we find the scales tipping over too much in one direction and we lose touch with the positive stream of thinking within us, it's time to retreat and regroup or we lose our sanity. The balancing act is necessary to bring us back to doing tasks effectively in a succinct, natural flow, without stress. Have a course of action for the day and work with a definite ending point in mind. This will help you work with ease and precision, keeping you on track.

August 19

ENCOURAGE—NEVER DISCOURAGE

Growing up, I was my harshest critic and brutal on myself my whole life, never knowing how to be gentle. Doing things with this attitude always set me up for failure. I put way too much pressure on myself, most times quitting and giving up. It made learning difficult for me and stopped the flow of my success. But when I started being around young children, I learned the value of gentleness. When a child is learning how to walk, the parents are very encouraging and cheer their child on as he or she begins to take those first steps. They are positive and praise their child for each small step taken. This fills the child with the encouragement, which I believe is the key to success in learning anything. The parents would never tell the child that they are a failure and uncoordinated, thus creating negative effects for their child. Instead, they guide her or him with gentleness and ease. I have adopted this way of learning for myself, and it has brought me success with inner peace. Now I encourage and *never* discourage myself. This approach to learning creates a healthy atmosphere to in which to learn—with gentleness as the guide.

August 20

MAKE IT A WIN-WIN

When we find ourselves ranting and raving about our own needs and not caring about what others need, we are being selfish in the extreme. *Gimme, gimme, gimme,* is the roll call of selfish people. If that sounds like you, then this may be why you are alone in life. Not wanting to give and digging our heels in at all costs causes irreparable rifts in relationships. But there is a solution to this, and it's called compromise—a win-win for both parties. We compromise when we reach a fair and equitable solution we can all agree on, one that allows each party to walk away a winner. You cannot build a relationship with an attitude of "What can you do for me?" Rather, healthy relationships are built on asking, "What can I do for you?" and "How can we help each other?" This is true compromise. Finding common ground and meeting in the middle will benefit all your relationships: marriage, friendships, employees, family members, or any interactions. Compromise for the win-win.

August 21

WHEN GOD REARRANGES THE FURNITURE

There are times in our lives when we are blindsided by sudden changes. These "punch-in-the-gut" moments, like unexpectedly losing your job or your partner deciding they no longer want to be married, shake us at our core and we are in shock and disbelief. We are left feeling very vulnerable with uncertainty and anxiety of what will happen next as we clamor for answers. We try to make sense of the events that make no sense and wonder why this is all happening to us. Whenever I'm faced with these obstacles, I know from my experience that these are the times when God is rearranging the furniture and changes are forthcoming. Everything in the room may look dismal and in disarray while we are made to wait as the Master decorator removes people, places, or things that no longer serve us or our highest good, producing something much better for us. As we let go and wait patiently for the results, we trust that God is doing for us what we could never do for ourselves and await our beautiful new room filled with new happiness.

August 22

THANK YOU FOR BEING HONEST

I thank God for the people who loved me enough to tell me the truth. Words cannot express my gratitude. Perhaps some of them are reading this now. I hope they all know who they are. Their honesty has helped light up my spirit by patiently helping me forge through layers of denial I had built up. Hearing the truth from these people emancipated me from the bondage of self I had created. I never knew who I was nor that I was capable of loving myself until others told me the truth about myself. These brave souls who courageously shared their own stories helped me identify what was wrong in my life. In turn, my life changed when I made the decision to live in truth too. Once you know the truth about yourself, you can never be the same again and I now share my life experiences to help others and strengthen the truth within me. I live my life as an open book and make self-honesty the most important thing in my life.

August 23

PUT IT ON THE SCALES

In life, we sometimes stress over insignificant things that are ridiculous and not worthy of a panic attack, like remembering where we left our keys or glasses, leaving no toilet paper in the bathroom, or leaving an empty milk carton in the fridge. These daily occurrences used to drive me up the wall and bring on full blown panic attacks. I threw away my peace and caused a lot of damage to my nervous system over trivial nonsense. I needed to chill out and pause, finding a better way to handle myself when these things would occur. Now, when these things happen, I take a deep breath and ask myself, How important is it? I then put everything in its proper perspective by using the scales of justice. On one scale, I put having an empty milk carton, and on the other scale, I put my sanity. I weigh them both to show myself how easy I give up my peace. Using the scales of justice has become a helpful tool to ground me. I now use this exercise in all areas of my life to help me get through whatever causes me stress. Put in on the scales of justice the next time you are confronted with stress and never let yourself lose it over toilet paper again.

August 24

DON'T BE A CLAM

If you don't speak up when someone is treating you wrong, your silence is saying it's right. Begin again and love yourself enough to change. Stand up for yourself and have the courage to speak up so others won't walk all over you. When the surf comes crashing down on clams, they shut down and quickly cover themselves by "clamming up." Don't be a clam. By playing small, you signal that you are weak and others will sense it and perhaps hurt you even more. You have a mighty force within you that needs to be nurtured by practicing courage and facing your fears. Call on that force by letting your voice be heard and turning your fear into faith, walking away with your head held high.

August 25

PLAN B FLEXIBLE

Routine sometimes lures us into a rut. We get so comfortable waking up knowing what we are going to do today, how, when, and with whom. Then, a sudden change comes into our lives—either by our choice or without our consent—and blindsides us. Responding to sudden change can be a struggle; we feel as if we are losing control, but the truth is, we never really had control. Control is an illusion we all buy into until we experience how powerless we really are. "Man plans and God laughs" is one of my all-time favorite expressions. There were countless times in my life when I planned things exactly the way I thought they should be, and I forged ahead thinking I was in control, and then everything turned out entirely different. The lesson is to make plans, but also be flexible. Always have a plan B and be open to the possibility that your best-laid plans may change. Above all, know that God will ultimately decide what's best for you. Just trust and be flexible.

August 26

HOLDING PATTERN

Is your life in a holding pattern? Sometimes planes are told to enter into a holding pattern because of congestion in the friendly skies. This keeps us safe while air traffic controllers go through a complex set of actions, ensuring all planes can come in for a smooth landing. Much like our lives, sometimes we are made to wait. God puts our life in a holding pattern while clearing up our present circumstances and planning our next move to make a better future for us. While we remain in our holding pattern, we can give thanks to our Creator and wait patiently in anticipation of the next chapter of our lives, knowing always we are in good hands.

August 27

LAUGHTER THROUGH TEARS

A good laugh can lighten any situation that is causing us turmoil.
Laughing through tears is the best medicine during tough times,
and I highly recommend it! I always thought that enjoying a comic
moment was unacceptable in the midst of grief or serious problems,
but I have found that the benefits of laughter are a necessary healing
balm. When I inject humor into any situation, I am on the way
to healing. Laughter is so good for the soul. I am blessed to have
a partner who is hilarious and always makes me laugh, especially
when I'm down. She is a Godsend and having her in my life is one of
God's gifts to me. Surround yourself with humor, and allow yourself
to laugh at something funny, whenever you have the chance. It will
chase away any sadness or grief, at least momentarily, lifting your
spirits during heavy situations.

August 28

HUMILITY HEALS ME

Without humility, I can never change. Humility is seeing your negative behaviors from the vantage point of truth and honesty, and making a decision to act better. Humility sees with truthful, objective, loving eyes. Humility corrects you as a good teacher might, speaking lovingly, gently correcting us with something like, "Good try, but do it this way," instead of shaming or being critical or judgmental. Humility will heal you with love. These humble moments of truth in my life come in a soft, loving whisper and I've come to see this is as the voice of God speaking. My Creator knows when I'm ready to listen and learn and that's when God speaks—firmly, but lovingly, giving me clarity, which is the grace of God spilling over me like pleasant rain. Cooling and cleansing humility is what I need to survive the new changes for the better occurring within me.

August 29

EXCUSES, EXCUSES

Excuses will ultimately do *you* in, not the real issue you are struggling
with. Excuses usually precede the issue and if you remove the excuses,
you can uncover the underlying problem and work to fix it. It's that
simple, but not easy. Sometimes we find ourselves making excuses all
day long and before we know it, we're spewing a list of reasons why
we didn't or can't do something, rationalizing just about anything.
In the end, you will see excuses stem from the many faces of fear.
Excuses cover up something we don't want to look at that is causing
us problems in our lives. Start identifying your excuses today; be
alert and notice when you try to excuse away your behavior. Instead,
get to the underlying issue. You can put a new plan into effect
without making excuses. You can make an excuse or you can make
an attempt to change.

August 30

SETTLE INTO YOUR JOY

When good changes are about to happen in our lives, anxiety often finds a way to creep in, shifting the focus to what could go wrong instead of allowing us to settle into our joy. Whether it's the birth of a new child, buying a new home, or starting a new job, fear makes an appearance even during happy occasions. Even when we are entering a new phase of our lives with only positive things happening, we still have some fear. Settle into your joy. Take a moment and realize where you were a year ago in your life and what is happening now! All your hard work is coming to fruition and is well-deserved. Feeding your mind with positive thoughts will drive your fears out. Start thinking of names for your new baby, what colors to paint the walls in your new home, or all the new associates you will meet at your new job. Let your new beginning arrive with all the joy it deserves.

August 31

SIBLINGS

Siblings are one of God's gifts. I have been blessed with three brothers who are all different, making our family diverse and interesting. My youngest brother is a talented musician who can play the guitar better than anyone. At five, he picked up a guitar and started playing, having never taken lessons! My middle brother is a talented actor, and an artist with a gift for drawing and painting. His work is magnificent! My oldest brother is an exceptional athlete who has won awards in multiple sports! I admire their special gifts from God and am very proud of them and all their accomplishments. Growing up, our mother taught us to watch out for and always support each other. This has become a constant theme into adulthood, knowing we will always be there for each other, family first. Our blood connects us, but our bonds are as strong as steel. I will always be grateful for my bros.

September 1

GOD DIDN'T DO IT

God is the source of only good in our lives, never bad. Blaming God for everything became fruitless when I found out *I* am responsible for my actions. There is no man in the sky handing out punishment, only our consequences do that. Becoming responsible for my thoughts first, then my actions, is what decides how my life plays out, good or bad. I create who and what I want to be by my thinking and when the "shit hits the fan," I need look no further than the mirror for the culprit. This is when I know, God didn't do it. I do it to myself.

September 2

A LITTLE TRUST

I used to think handing my life over to God was like handing over my dog or a baby to a stranger. In the beginning of my search for faith, it was a struggle trusting in anything I couldn't see or feel and the idea of God was strange to me. All I ever really trusted was myself. But my life was out of control and I had to start trusting in *something* greater than myself. At first, I leaned on other people and their guidance; I saw them and their journey to faith as something greater than me, and that led me to my own understanding of God. I followed their example, tried what they did, and found my own faith by practicing spiritual principles. Now, when I find myself in a tough spot, I easily give it over to God to put the pieces back together for me. I have no more doubt and am blessed with a faith that allows me to stand firm in the face of some tough experiences, knowing I am never alone as long as I trust God.

September 3

BOOMERANG

Do you pay close attention to how you speak to and act toward others? Try it today and see what you learn and how observing yourself can alter your words and actions. This experiment will change your life for the better. Until I began to observe myself in dealing with others, I never knew how much of an attitude I had and how often it got me into trouble. Take a look and watch how you treat people. Our treatment of others is like a boomerang. What you give out, you will get back. It's that simple. I know from experience that if I'm confronted with nasty people all day, it's time for me to step back and check my own behavior and ask myself, "Am *I* being nasty?" Most times, it's a yes. When I spread nastiness, that's what boomerangs back to me. But I can also spread love and get love back. This is a choice we can always make and it's so much easier to be nice. Boomerang yourself into being a better person.

September 4

GHOSTING

Where are you? Why don't you call? Are you ignoring me? "Ghosting" your friends fills their heads with so many questions about you and your suddenly disappearing behavior; they begin to second guess your friendship. If you are sometimes in and sometimes out, not answering texts, calls, or emails for long periods of time, you are ghosting! Whether intentional or not, ghosting others is shady behavior that breaks down trust between two people and trust is the basis of all good relationships. Start answering, it's that simple. Let them know all is well. True friendship is a connection that never breaks and is reciprocal. Check in and be available. If there's an issue bothering you, be mature and bring it up for discussion—like a human instead of a ghost.

September 5

REARVIEW MIRROR

Sometimes when we make mistakes, we're tempted to sit on the self-pity pot, stewing. This only keeps you in the problem. Don't stay stuck in the past and grieve over mistakes you made and can't change. Move forward now. Starting over is part of our journey—stops and starts, letdowns and setbacks. Beginning again is how we take responsibility for our mistakes and grow smarter. Sure, you can look back at the past, but do so as if glancing in the rearview mirror of your car, then bringing your eyes right back to the road ahead. Use the experience to see what changes need to be made going forward, put it in the rearview mirror, and drive away to a better future.

September 6

KEEP IT SIMPLE

Keeping things simple is always best. When we are faced with any task, simplicity should be in the forefront. When we complicate our plans with our complicated minds, we screw things up. If I have a lot to do, my mind can become scattered with a thousand thoughts, like bees swarming in my head. When I overcomplicate things, I block any creative flow needed for my project. Instead of seeing the simple actions I need to take, I become paralyzed by how difficult the task seems. That's when I need to stop and start again. Now, I always say a prayer before I start any big task: *God, please let divine mind flow through me now.* Bringing God into the equation clears away any static and refocuses my mind, so I can approach any project in a more organized manner. I get the clarity needed without the stress and can work while at peace, keeping it simple.

September 7

PEACE TO PAIN

Ok, so you didn't listen to direct instructions given by a professional. Instead, you decided to do it your way, perhaps in the name of love and with good motives. But the choice you made blew up in your face and now you're paying the price. Sometimes when we take things into our own hands, ignoring wiser counsel, we can go from peace to pain in an instant. Riddled with guilt, we ask ourselves over and over, "WHY? Things were going so smoothly!" In my case, I know that throwing a wrench into a perfect situation is always because of me thinking I know best. Unfortunately, these are painful life lessons we all experience and there is no cure for this other than remembering what happened in the past when you thought you knew better than others. Before you decide on your own, better to think it through to the possible consequences. Stop and think before you act, ensuring a peaceful outcome.

September 8

CAN YOU DIG IT?

I don't need your approval to be me. What a freedom it is to know this finally, to understand that what others think of me means nothing to me. I have been at peace with myself ever since I've come to know this. I wish this peace and clarity for all. For a long time, I struggled with seeking approval and that insecurity got in the way of relationships. But eventually I had enough of being in bondage and began to change my outlook. This state of mind doesn't come easily or just happen. My new attitude developed over time and through much hard work. Letting go and standing alone with my truth was scary, but I pierced through that veil of fear and now it will never hurt me or hinder me again. I'm strong and secure within myself and no longer pay attention to what others think of me. I've achieved a major new mindset, like digging a gold mine. You dig and dig and dig every day, hoping. When you no longer struggle with what others think, you've struck gold.

September 9

OFF LIKE A DIRTY SHIRT

Jesus said, beware of wolves in sheep's clothing. In business and personal relationships, I have had to become aware of this to protect myself. Wolves in disguise do walk among us every day, waiting for their prey to appear. Sometimes spotting phony people is difficult; they smile sweetly to your face while concocting a plan for your demise. Have you ever encountered such a person? I try to first give everyone the benefit of the doubt until I see otherwise. But when I see the phony appear, I'm off like a dirty shirt! If you stay, you run the risk of getting hurt and will have no one to blame but yourself. Don't be fooled, listen to the ancient wise words: "If it's too good to be true, then it is." Trust your gut in relationships and be cautious. Only when others' words match their actions, may you begin to trust. Works every time.

September 10

FANCY PANTS

When prosperity comes into our life, all of a sudden, BOOM! Our egos blow up and we may start acting like a fancy pants, no longer saying a simple hello to others, thinking they should acknowledge us first. We become too important and see others as beneath us. Remember this truth: no matter how well-off you are or what status or power you hold, you are no better than anyone else. It's wise to remember where you came from because you can easily return there. Fortunes can change in a minute and we can be left broke and homeless. Then who will you be? It is our saving grace that God loves us all the same no matter how much cash we have, what job we hold, how popular or powerful we are. So, stay grounded. Continue doing for others and showing kindness to all. As long as we stay humble, we create more goodness in our own lives and the lives of others.

—

September 11

PLANT LOVE IN THE ASHES

Each year when this day arrives, I'm reminded of the horrific acts
of terrorism against our country. Many good people died that day
just because they went to work. A few of them were people I grew
up with, and for years I could not shake my anger and outrage. But
over time, this changed and my thinking is much clearer now: I
know I cannot hold a whole country, religion, or region of the world
accountable for the despicable acts of a few. The sadness I felt for
a very long time has healed and turned into a somber respect for
all life. I realized God would want me to love in spite of the hatred
in the world. So, on this day, I plant love in the ashes. I spend the
day sharing love and blessings with everyone I meet, performing a
random act of kindness and letting that spread around the world. Try
it. Let this day be about love and healing, each of us doing our part,
one person at a time, to change the world.

September 12

OPPOSITE DAY

If you're struggling with ill feelings for another, just for today, do something different about that. If your natural inclination is to act out of that negativity, try doing the opposite. Declare today "Opposite Day." The boss is getting on your nerves and you have been tearing him apart in your head all day? Try blessing him instead. Your co-worker is acting cold? Bless them for they are likely fighting a battle we know nothing about. Do you listen to the news in the car on the way to work and feel anxious? Try no radio and instead offer up a prayer for everyone you see in the other cars. You can be free if you want. You just have to do the opposite. Practice this remedy today and watch as good things start happening. Wouldn't it be wonderful if we as a nation declare one day a month "Opposite Day?" I believe we can change the world with this small action.

September 13

COME-AS-YOU-ARE PARTY

God will meet you exactly where you are in life with whatever baggage and problems you're currently carrying. That's how much you are loved by your Creator. That's how it happened for me so why not everyone! If you are searching for faith, come as you are. You need not worry about changing who you are first, for that is fruitless. None of us can change without God's power and help anyway; this is why we seek God in the first place. So, bring all your hurts, fears, problems, and addictions to God. It's a come-as-you-are party. God accepts us all wherever we are in consciousness and helps us in our struggles. However, once we receive the gift of faith, it's not a stay-as-you-are party; then it's time for us to do the work on ourselves and glorify God's power.

September 14

MY SPECIAL FRIEND

Friends help us see the best in ourselves and others. They are gifts from God, there to pick us up when we feel down or share in our successes. I have one friend who is very special, and we have shared many years of laughter and tears together. Sharyn has seen me at my best and at my worst and remained by my side through it all. I cherish our friendship and am blessed to have her in my life. Our bond is stronger than steel and no person or problem can ever come between us. She is the sister I never had. Whether blood relative or not, we share the same commitment to support each other throughout our lives. Relationships like these are rare and when you find them or they find you, hold on forever, remembering to thank God for the gift of a special friendship.

September 15

IT'S NOT ABOUT YOU

The unconditional love of pets brings so much joy to our lives. But, with all that joy, there are responsibilities as well. When you make the decision to own a pet, you become a caretaker for the rest of that animal's life. Properly feeding them, grooming, exercising, loving and playing with them, vet visits when they are sick, and keeping them healthy are all part of the responsibilities. But, the biggest and most difficult caretaking task is when they become sick and can no longer go on. You must be ready to do what is right for them. It's not about you. Saying goodbye is the most unselfish act I have ever needed to carry out. Making the decision was heartbreaking, but it gave peace to their soul. When I said goodbye to my dogs, I held them and whispered how much I loved and appreciated them being in my life. This fulfilled a promise I made to them when they came into my life, that my face would be the last thing they saw on this earth and I would never leave their side when it was their time to go to God. I gave them the peace and unselfish love they deserved.

September 16

YOUR SPIRITUAL BANK ACCOUNT

It's important to save money. Everyone needs to secure funds for that rainy day, which is a wise practice that will help us somewhere down the road. But what about our spiritual bank account? Did you know you have one of those too? Filling it with love will secure your needs down the road too. Take time to love. In the end, love is the only thing we leave behind. Not our jewelry, cars, houses, or money, but our good deeds, unselfish acts, and kind words. Nothing but the love you give and share with others, freely, will feed your spirit and fill your spiritual bank account. Having a healthy spiritual bank account also fills us with tremendous happiness, knowing that by helping others and depositing love, our own needs will always be met. Make a deposit into your spiritual bank account today by spreading love to everyone, especially someone who needs it.

September 17

BE REAL

People see your actions, but God knows your motives. Be authentic. You were created free to be whoever you are. Bring your beauty out and let the world see what God has created. Start by letting your words and deeds match. However difficult or afraid you may be today, speak your truth, act your truth. Practice self-honesty until it becomes automatic. Honest people are always at ease with themselves since they have nothing to hide and make others feel safe to do the same. Honesty is contagious. Others will open up and be real as you show them by your example. By living an honest life, you will attract honest people and know what true freedom to be yourself really means.

September 18

MAKE A SPIRITUAL CONNECTION

Make a spiritual connection by taking the time to listen to others when they are hurting. If someone needs to share their burdens, listen with an open heart and without judgment. Being there for others will uplift you both with this unselfish act of kindness and love. I feel the closest to God when bearing witness to others and I walk away with a profound sense of peace and humility. We all need to be heard and this healing act will not only heal others but you as well. It helps you remember that in your dark times others were there for you. By sharing our strength with others, we forge a spiritual connection for life.

September 19

PEACEFUL MOTIVATION

I never understood how motivating people in the workplace through fear would bring out the best in them. Being in office meetings listening to a boss yelling at me and threatening me to perform never motivated me and never will. Motivation through fear doesn't work and, in fact, will do the opposite. I will pull my foot off the gas. Standing over your employees and putting them under a microscope will only lead to them making more mistakes because now the pressure is on. We become tense and feel we need to compete with others, rather than focus on getting our job done. The act of pitting people against each other is so primitive and destroys good will among the employees. In contrast, creating a calm and relaxed space in which employees can work will lessen their tension and might just inspire them to go above and beyond the call of duty. If you're workplace is tension-filled or hostile, it may be time to explore your options of finding a friendly work environment that will be better for your health and sanity.

September 20

OFFER PRAYER

When family, friends, or even strangers would go through difficult times, I used to feel so helpless wishing there was something I could do for them. As I watched them suffer through their ordeal, it became my heartache too as a piece of me would hurt. My nephew had open heart surgery when he was five months old, and it was a very tough time for my entire family. I remember the pain and fear on everyone's faces and wished I could take it away. It was then that I realized the only thing I could do is pray for them. Offering prayers to God for healing and strength not only helped my family but was what held *me* up. Placing them all under God's loving protection and care gave me great comfort and helped me be strong for them. Praying for others is something we can all do at any time. Offering prayers of healing and strength in the midst of difficult times means we don't have to feel helpless, but helpful.

September 21

LOVE IS THE ANSWER

We speak of love as something we make, something we take, and something we give. But what about love as the answer to any problem we encounter in our lives? Have you considered that love is the answer to *any* question? Love can heal any situation, if we choose it. When we lead with love and insert love in our lives, a host of questions are often automatically answered. If I am at odds with a sibling, I start giving love instead of attitude and I make peace with my brother instead of pushing him away. If my partner is cranky, I give kindness and am generous of spirit and watch the crankiness fade from her face. Love will always win. Start putting this practice to the test in your life. More love in any situation will heal it. No matter what the question, love is the answer.

September 22

CHOOSE YOUR HARD

The struggle we experience when trying to overcome something in our lives can be very difficult some days. Whatever you're going through, there are days when you'll want to throw in the towel. When I first quit smoking, some days the urge to smoke was with me 24/7. Many times, I wanted to give up and take the easy way out, lighting up again, justifying or ignoring my commitment to quit. What I found is I had to push on and take action in spite of wanting to smoke. Doing nothing, complaining, or rationalizing a return to the bad habit will only lead you backward. Change is hard. Going forward is hard. But going back to something that will kill me or allowing it to continue would be even worse. Choose your hard. You will struggle for a while but then the climb gets easier. Push forward with all you have and God will bring you through. Turning back will delay the freedom that awaits you.

September 23

GRIEF HAS NO TIMELINE

There is no handbook to refer to when someone you love passes away. Grief has no timeline to follow, no expiration date; grief is a profound process of letting go and only you can decide when and how to move through your particular grief. You must allow yourself to grieve in whatever way feels right, without judgment from yourself or others. Give grief the time it requires. The time you need when enduring a loss can be so very painful, at times you may feel like you can't breathe. Some days I have to break time down into smaller increments to endure the pain of grief. One moment at a time is all I can bear. Then I gradually get to one hour at a time, and one day at a time to find some strength in the midst of all my grief. As this time frame grows, the heaviness of grief lifts. And so begins my healing, in time.

September 24

BE BOLD

When it's time to make your move, be bold. Walk like you own the place. Don't let fear hold you back. Bold people seem to get all the breaks because they speak their minds without fear of losing anything, but rather knowing they have much to gain. This bold mindset is one you must prepare yourself to embrace each day. It may not feel natural, though it gets easier as you practice proudly taking bold actions. Don't accept the status quo. If you have something to say, say it. If you have something to do, do it. Say a prayer and bring God into it, a mighty force to help you. What's the worst thing that could happen? Lives can change, especially yours—if you step up and be bold.

September 25

LIFE FINDS A WAY

It may rain, but the sun will shine again. Life may look bleak but always finds a way to turn itself around again. Never think your current situation is all there is. You are not stuck. The only dead ends in life are in your mind. In reality, life finds a way. There may be crossroads we will have to face but a way forward always appears. The ride may be rough at times and there will almost certainly be detours, but that road will become smooth again as you continue on your journey. Always remember life finds a way and God will lead you and guide you there. Hold fast to your faith and keep going straight ahead, never turning back and remembering… life finds a way.

September 26

I CALL IT GOD

There is a power within me that does for me what I cannot do for myself. Awakening that power, through a lot of pain, has been a most bittersweet experience. Through my suffering, I have found I am much more than whatever I am experiencing when I make contact with this power. This I do daily through prayer and meditation, which has become my ritual. I have a well of strength, love, and intuition at the core of my being, as we all do, and I call this God. When I began soul-searching, looking for answers, I had no conception of what a loving God was, and didn't like what had been pushed on me by my childhood religion lessons. Then one day, someone told me they used this acronym for God: *Good Orderly Direction.* Why not have a God of my own understanding making the idea of God personal to me? So, I began to use this description as well. Living my life with *Good Orderly Direction* is living God's will and I am protected and at peace. When I made the connection from my head to my heart, I found this inner power. Today, when I feel lost or I'm going through tough times, I use this prayer: *God, help me to find you at the center of my being.* This helps me remember I am not alone and God is only a breath away.

September 27

PERFECTLY IMPERFECT

Are you perfectly imperfect? That's okay. You can say it. You're not alone because none of us are perfect. Perfection lies in the heavens above and while we can strive for perfection, in our human existence we can never fully achieve perfection. We get glimmers of it, at some times more than others, but we all have to be content with being perfectly imperfect. Every human makes mistakes. Once I really accepted this fact, it made my life easier. We put so much pressure on ourselves to perform to perfection, placing unrealistic demands upon ourselves, which causes us pain. Today, I set my goals and try my best—that's it. When I fall short of my desired goals, I remind myself that tomorrow is another day when I can try again. I keep it simple and do not throw myself into a tantrum by setting unreasonable demands. I remind myself, I am perfectly imperfect.

September 28

BRING THE LIGHT

Just because it's a gloomy day outside doesn't mean we have to be in a gloomy mood. Turn on your inner light and let it shine as brightly as the sun. Bring that glow to all you meet today and become the light in another's life. Sometimes just a smile and a sunny attitude is all it takes to help brighten another's dark mood. Many people are fighting personal battles in life and need any love you can share with a cheerful, sunny disposition. All darkness fades when you turn on the light for others. With this attitude, the light blesses us and others and helps make the world a happier place.

September 29

NO WHINING

Are you whining about something? Well, whining only makes your problems worse and will never solve anything. Yes, it's helpful to discuss your problems and get them out in the open, but then make the changes necessary to fix them without complaining. Pick yourself up and begin again. Be a part of the solution, not the problem. When you identify with the problem and keep whining about it, you stay stuck. Try to remember there are so many people worse off than you are. Perhaps your problems are luxury problems when compared to theirs. Make the decision right now to stop the pity party and begin taking the steps to fix whatever is wrong. If someone you know and care about is whining, ask, "Would you like some cheese with that whine?" With this playful phrase, you can try to snap them—or maybe even yourself—out of it. It works!

September 30

LIVE AND LET LOVE

Love with no barriers, restrictions, rules, or judgment. Just love! We were created free to love whomever we choose; that is between us and our God. This is one of the greatest freedoms of our generation and it's not up for debate or discussion by the masses. No one person or group of people have the monopoly on love and how it's shared, in spite of what they may think. Putting love in a box and labeling it doesn't make the world a better place, but only confuses people who are already confused. Why not just support love? Live and let love! Since each of us is different, dictating others' lifestyles and pretending to know what's good for another only leads to separation in society. Supporting each other is supporting love. Let's all come together and let others decide what's best for them, choosing who they want to love. Support love, not who or how we should love. Simply live and let love.

October 1

CHANGES

As I write today's message while sitting in my backyard on a beautiful, crisp day, I'm reminded of how things change without our consent. Automatically, we go from one season to the next. Just a few short weeks ago we were swimming in the pool and barbecuing in the hot summer sun. Now I sit and watch colorful leaves falling from the trees with the autumn chill in the air caressing me. Everything changes. Nothing ever stays the same. This idea of constant change can be comforting when we go through tough times, facing challenges we never experienced. Or it can be sad when things are good and we never want them to end. But everything *will* change, everything has an ending. Such is life. Change is the one constant in the universe. Learning to accept change and finding the silver lining are life skills we continue to strive toward and get better at each with each new experience.

October 2

OBSESSIONS

At some point, we all obsess about things we have no control over
and it can rule our lives, making us miserable. Our minds and
thought processes are very powerful and can be used to either help
us or hurt us, depending on the thoughts we feed ourselves. Whether
it's a substance, a relationship, a medical outcome, or fear and
anxiety about the future, they can all crowd our minds and become
obsessions. Too much fear about the future can put us into a full-
blown panic attack, and replaying past hurts brings depression or we
become guilt ridden. The more you feed them, the more powerful
they become. We are seduced into a state of delusion by our egos
that tricks us into thinking we are ok when, in fact, it has you in its
powerful grip. When we suffer enough, we look for the way out, and
whether of not it is clear to you, you do have a choice. Stop feeding
an outdated image of yourself that is connected to the old self you
loathe and become new. Change means doing things differently, and
it starts with your thinking. This is the way to a new self. Push out all
negative thoughts of yesterday and tomorrow and feed off only good
thoughts in the present. Flood your mind with the positive things in
life you are grateful for and begin your transformation.

October 3

Dig Yourself

Finding true happiness is no longer being a size six. That ship sailed for me a long time ago and I have come to accept my body size and dig myself exactly the way I am. Thankfully, my perception of happiness has changed and the things I thought I needed to be happy have lost their meaning. True happiness is a journey and making the decision to be happy is a choice you make. It doesn't arrive on your doorstep without doing the footwork. Being happy stems from an attitude of gratitude that you cultivate throughout all facets of your life. It's being humble and content with all you have and needing nothing, accepting everything exactly the way it is with a live and let live mindset, knowing you are only one among many. We experience this serenity when we choose to love ourselves. I am fulfilled, blessed, and yes, I really dig myself!

October 4

STEP UP OR STEP AWAY?

Think about that look on someone's face when you say something nice to them and help turn their day around. Or, the act of being there for someone who is struggling or frightened. These gratifying moments in life, when we feel better because we helped others, expecting nothing in return, define our character. Who do you want to be? When you have an opportunity to help someone, will you step up or step away? Choosing to step up is not easy sometimes but always fulfilling. Being there for others when they are afraid or alone is what our Creator expects of us. Open your heart and look inside. There is much love within you and expressing it will bring you much love in return. Step up and give of yourself. Be a healing light in someone else's darkness. Step up and experience your own spiritual fulfillment.

October 5

GOD SCHEDULED THE MEETING

Today, I took my dog for a leisurely walk like I do every day. But this day, I met a guy who was suffering from the recent loss of his dog. Sadly, I have experienced this several times in my life with much heartache but have come through the other side. As he is telling me about his experience, all I can think of is, there are no coincidences. God placed him directly in my path for a reason so I could deliver a message of hope during his difficult time of loss and grief. The calming, loving words I spoke seemed to give him some relief that things would get better over time. God scheduled the meeting with this stranger who needed to hear what I had to say. This was no chance encounter; my words were just in time. God's timing is incredible, and God connects us to others when we are most needed. God is scheduling meetings between people all day every day to help us get through struggles. Many times in my life people showed up at exactly the right time with a message of hope to fill me with the strength I needed. We are here to learn our lessons and then to share our experiences to help others overcome theirs. Whether it is a casual encounter or an introduction through acquaintances, God will schedule the meeting.

October 6

HIT THAT CURVEBALL

Never be afraid when something new is being added to your life. Accept and embrace it. Resistance produces anxiety, so let changes flow into your life. They are happening for a reason. Perhaps you have outgrown your current situation and it no longer serves your highest good. God knows this and is bringing you a new beginning. It reminds me of my days playing softball. Every good hitter knows they should be ready for all types of pitches and prepares accordingly. Sometimes the pitch is a curveball. So do what a good hitter does: wait on the pitch, adjust your swing, and hit it out of the park. Curveballs can be a good thing if they propel you to a more positive outcome. So, hold on to your faith and let the changes come.

October 7

ONE AMONG MANY

Throughout my life, I aspired to be the best in everything I did. Conquer the world! It's a good thing to desire to be the best in all you do. But at what cost? When this pressure spills into hurting ourselves and others, that's where this attitude goes awry. I stepped on and over people to get what I wanted, struggling to get to the top of the heap. But once I arrived, I wanted to hide underneath it. The pendulum would swing both ways and either I was too good for something or not good enough. Never could I find the in-between, the middle ground. After a series of crashing and burning and being sick and tired of hurting myself, I found it's not a race. Life is not about getting to the top, but about how I treat others along the way. Living with integrity, as but one among many, living with honesty, kindness and love will always get me further in life and also allows me to be a source of good to those around me. When I leave the house with an attitude of being one among many, I attract the love and goodness from others that I need to survive and thrive in the world. I bring out the best in others as well as myself.

October 8

WHEN THEY SAY NO

I didn't know how pushy or controlling I was until someone sat me down and told me to chill. It was an eye-opener and I'm grateful to that person for helping me change. No one wants to be controlled. When a person tries to control another, it destroys relationships. Spotting this behavior is the only chance we have to be able to change it. Control is insidious and has many disguises. One of the ways your need to control will infiltrate your life without you even noticing is when you ask someone if they need your help and they reply "no" but you continue to push, insisting you want to help them. This is your control issue emerging, not you trying to help. This is a perfect example of a bad motive hiding underneath a good one. But it's there nonetheless and becoming aware is important so you can change your behavior. Each day I make an effort to not push others and remind myself that when I hear "No" it means no. I stop asking and can then let others be.

October 9

FIND YOUR TOP

Falling in love is such a magical time in our lives. I believe that in the universe there is, according to an old expression, a lid for every pot. When we fall in love, we finally find our missing top. I have been blessed to experience this phenomenon in my life with my partner. God sent her into my life exactly at the right time. If you are lucky enough to meet the right person and share romantic love, hold on and nurture it. You will have someone in your corner, through thick and thin, someone to weather challenging times at your side, who cares about you and loves you unconditionally. The connection is deep on many levels as you join together and become one, sharing your lives. After 20 years together, I still get excited when I see her name come up on a text or phone call! Betty Ann is the love of my life. We celebrate our love for each other by making the best of every situation, finding humor and a silver lining in all things.

October 10

PULL OFF THE BANDAGE

Leaving relationships is very painful, much like pulling off the bandage off a wound. You know it's gonna hurt like hell but have to do it. I was very unhappy in a relationship and was becoming more miserable, sinking into a pit of depression that only got deeper. I wanted to leave but did not want to hurt the other person, staying much longer than I should have. This hurt *me* tremendously. But finally, after much pain and suffering, I left. God gave me the strength to do what was right for me and seek the happiness I wanted for myself. Having to end a relationship because things don't work out is okay. People change and sometimes find they no longer have enough in common. Staying in a relationship when both are unhappy and your needs are not met is not okay. Doing the right thing for ourselves through self-care and self-love is what God expects of us so we may live free and find our happiness. We are not responsible for the happiness of others at the expense of our own. Each of us must find that happiness for ourselves first and that sometimes requires letting go.

October 11

YES, I CAN!

Some days I feel as though the mountain moves me rather than me moving mountains. Those are the days I try to do life on my own willpower instead of turning to God for strength to get me through. I can do nothing on my own, for God does the work through me when I align myself with God's power. By surrendering to what is happening at the moment and asking God to help me, I bring a mighty force that *can* move mountains. I walk in faith through my day with God by my side and the unseen does for me what I cannot do for myself. "Yes, I can!" becomes my mantra and I am restored to the state of fearlessness I yearn for and begin to move those mountains once again.

October 12

No Time Like Now

Do you have unfinished business? Whether work responsibilities, a personal project, or just a phone call you need to make, why not finish it today? Take aim and then follow through. Putting it off is procrastination and when procrastination gets the best of you, it will fester and expand to other areas of your life. Put the finishing touches on your neglected project. Our time here on earth is never promised to us, so complete the thing that has been dangling in your mind. Completing projects is greatly rewarding and the satisfaction will inspire more great accomplishments. Once you touch that spark of creativity, it will start you in a new direction—maybe even a new life.

October 13

IF YOU DON'T SAY IT'S WRONG, YOU'RE SAYING IT'S RIGHT

What you give your consent to is what you become. If something is wrong and you don't stand up for what is right, you are part of the problem. You have given your consent without speaking a word! When everything and everyone around you stands against you, try this: stand up. The stakes may be high, but own your truth in spite of what others think. Hold your head high and speak your truth directly to their souls. Speaking your truth and conveying this knowledge is what makes you who you are. Waking others up from their deep slumber is something God expects of us and a blessing we can share with others. They may not like it or they may thank you, but the results are not yours to judge. Only God can judge. By your example, others will learn the value of standing up and it may spur them to do the same when it counts in their lives. Say what needs to be said and leave it there for God to work out.

October 14

TELL YOUR STORY

Tell your story. Someone needs to hear it. We all go through challenging times that bring us to the breaking point, only to come back stronger. Tell others how you weathered difficulties; be an inspiration. The valuable knowledge we gained about ourselves during our own struggles needs to be shared with others to help them through their darkness. Finding out we are so much more than we thought we were at defining moments needs to be shouted from the rooftops so we can help others who are struggling on the path. When we share these miracles of perseverance in the service of helping and inspiring others, more miracles arrive. I have been blessed in my lifetime with many miracles that began with others sharing their stories. My life is a testament that faith and hard work will change any situation and I now love telling *my* story of transformation to anyone who will listen.

October 15

Consistency Is the Key

Without consistency, we can never reach our goals. With an on-again off-again attitude, we make attempts but can never finish anything or enact real change within ourselves. Aiming to change is difficult and sometimes we go to war with ourselves, but the benefits are miraculous. The daily battles are painful and at times and we want to give up, but we must push on if we want to become new. Some days this is a daily grind, painfully going through the motions. Other days are easier and we are connected to the part of us that sincerely wants to change. Staying your course requires commitment. When you attempt to quit anything, it helps to have a constant visual reminder of why you want that change. When I was first trying to quit smoking, I had to devise a daily visual wake-up call, so I started the day by looking at a picture of a diseased lung riddled with lung cancer. I kept it front and center and carried it with me all over the place, especially on those difficult days. I needed something drastic that would slap me out of my slumber when I was attempting to rationalize having a cigarette. Because of that image, I'd remember the pain I was brought to from smoking and woke up again. Consistency has saved my life. When we want to change, there are no half measures. Freedom can only be obtained through eternal vigilance. We must walk, talk, eat, sleep, and think differently to effect change in ourselves.

October 16

LEAD WITH LOVE

Imagine if we could all lead with love today? The whole world making a conscious effort to put love first in all their affairs. Wars would end, suffering and hunger gone, nations would be at peace, and we could all experience the true camaraderie of humanity as God wants. Our world could become a safe place and we would all be proud to live in it. So, do it. Lead with love. If enough of us can do this, others will follow our lead. Love is contagious and the effects would be felt around the world. Let love be your guiding force and we will all live at peace with each other. Simply, this is how we change the world.

October 17

WHAT IS LOVE?

What is love? Ever think about that? Give it some careful thought right now. What does love mean to you? Some say love is indescribable. Though we each have our own definition and individual experiences to draw from, certainly we can all agree that love is a blissful state of mind—a euphoric feeling brought on when I see someone I love, I look at my dog, or listen to a beautiful song with lyrics I can relate to. When my four-year-old nephew Cooper shows me his latest dance moves, my heart explodes with love. But there are other ways love shows up. Helping someone who is down find their way, listening to a friend who needs an ear or shoulder to cry on, or being kind to strangers. These acts unleash feelings of love and once love is released, it creates empathy for others, one of the greatest experiences of love. Love's healing touch is what's needed in our world today and if each of us would just show a portion of love, we could change our world dramatically.

October 18

LIKE VERSUS LOVE

"You don't have to like them, but you have to love them." A very
good friend of mine uttered these words to me a long time ago
and it changed my life once I realized the difference. Now I never
confuse those two words and know what God expects of me. While
it's not possible to like everyone you meet—our personalities are all
different and that's okay—we must love them anyway, meaning we
should treat everyone in a loving, kind way. We don't need to invite
them over for dinner, just come from a loving place when interacting
with them. Each of us are fingers on a hand in God's kingdom, all
of us brothers and sisters, and all of our fellow "siblings" deserve
this respect. Holding good loving thoughts about others, without
judgment, keeps me in a peaceful place while having ill feelings wears
away at the core of my being. So, keep it light when in the company
of those whose company you may not enjoy. Remember, you don't
have to like them, but you have to love them.

October 19

THE HIGH ROAD

Take the high road today—especially if it's not your normal response. Try creating a new normal by doing the right thing the first time, until it becomes automatic. The rewards will be worth it. The road of honesty, integrity, and kindness is paved with riches beyond this world for all who seek it. I never go without when I'm on this high road; all my needs are always met. I build a world where I give to others—and thus can receive back—love, respect, and kindness. When traveling the high road, effortlessly my life falls into place. I begin to see the beauty in people, and my fears and judgments are pushed away by something far bigger than myself. I am surrounded by the peace that dwells within my soul and I am *in* the world but not *of* this world. The high road leads to heaven on earth for me, my nirvana.

October 20

FAIL, BUT NEVER A FAILURE

If someone makes a mistake, what is your response? Do you react with love or judgment? We have much to learn about ourselves from the way we interact with others. It's a split-second choice we make, and it can either make or break a relationship. Responding with judgment will always turn people off, add to their guilt, make them feel like a failure, and begs them to retaliate. Nothing is learned and you have created a rift in your relationship that may never be repaired, with ill feelings remaining. However, when the response to a mistake is love and compassion, others are more apt to listen and learn from what transpired; we allay their feelings of guilt, instead of piling on more. We build them up rather than tear them down. We should be mindful that all people, including ourselves, will fail but should never be made to feel like a failure. Love and compassion are the greatest teachers. Everyone makes mistakes and how we respond will make a difference in whether we are perceived as teaching or preaching. Become aware of your reactions and make the necessary changes to become more compassionate toward others when they fail.

October 21

SPEAK YOUR MIND

Loyalty is admirable in all forms, but loyalty to the truth should be first and foremost. Speaking your truth and expressing your opinion are two of the greatest freedoms we have in life. Society is in warring fragments because people will not speak up and we unnecessarily suffer because of those who are disloyal to the truth. Here is an acid test: Do you vote along party lines or for the best candidate? Will you go along with others so that you keep your friends? Would you advocate for the right thing even if it makes you unpopular? Having the courage to side with your conscience isn't easy, but it will lead you to your highest good. Align yourself with truth and you will be aligning yourself with God. Speak your mind. Make your voice heard among the masses.

October 22

STAY GROUNDED

All we have is the present moment. We cannot change what happened yesterday nor can we control what is about to happen. Staying grounded in the present is the only way we can make decisions to shape our future and heal from our past. The present can erase past regrets if we adopt new ways of doing things to ensure different outcomes. Staying grounded in the present also keeps us from the anxiety we feel when our thoughts drift to the future, imagining scenarios that may never come to pass. My mental health depends on staying in the moment, which I consciously practice all day, every day. You can begin a new regimen for your mental health today by keeping yourself grounded in the present—the only place where true happiness and peace can be found.

October 23

THE INN IS FULL

Are your prayers being answered? If not, the reason could be that it's too crowded in your life, stuffed with too much that doesn't belong there. When I pray and ask God for all that I want, I must also make myself ready to receive those new people, situations, or things by creating space. Once I realized this, I started taking stock and removing the old, the unwanted, the broken, or outgrown things that didn't serve my highest good anymore, making a place for the new to arrive. When I wanted a new relationship, I had to remove Miss Wrong so the universe could deliver Miss Right. When the inn is full, nothing new can enter. Start taking inventory of what's already in your life but may be impeding your good from arriving. Then, begin the process of letting go and put up the "vacancy" sign.

October 24

JUST LET

In tennis, a "let" occurs when a small error is allowed to go by without impeding the progress of the game. When we allow a let in life, we give in to what is happening around us right that second and move on. When we don't allow the let, we push, we make mistakes, and we have regrets. So, just let. Don't push. Allow this tiny word to guide you. Follow God's lead by surrendering to what is. God has a plan all ready for you; your job is to show up and step up into God's plan each day. Just let it unfold naturally and organically and you will be brought to where you need to be. That's the power of the let.

October 25

WHEN GOD SHOWS UP

If you're not sure there is a God, think again and hear this: Either God is or I'm an illusion. Here's what I mean. God showed up in my life at exactly the right moment. I was about to jump off a building, desperate, without hope and wanting to end it all quickly. My demons got the best of me and life became too hard. Thankfully, I called a friend who loves me and she literally talked me off the roof. In retrospect, I see it was the voice of God that saved me, speaking through my friend. The spoken words of love were more powerful than my demons and they saved my life, piercing through the darkness and denial in me and pulling me back to life. I will always be grateful to my friend, but I now know it was God doing for me what I could never do for myself. I should've died that day, but for the grace of God, I'm here. When God shows up in your life you will know it too. In an instant, everything changes and you are reborn as a sense of peace and fulfillment comes over you. It's a deep understanding within your soul that all will be well in spite of whatever you are going through. Reaching out to others is reaching out to God. Find someone to confide in and God will show up.

October 26

ADVERSITY SHOWS YOU—YOU!

Adversity introduces us to ourselves. Just when you think you have nothing left in the tank, God shows you how resilient you truly are. The human spirit cannot be broken when aligned with God's grace. We all have an unlimited supply of faith and strength within us waiting to be tapped. Going on in spite of stressful challenges is difficult, but if you quit you will never experience how strong you really are! Unleash your power within during tough times by calling on God for strength. It will lead you out of your difficulties and deliver you from yourself just when you think you are spent. Hold on, keep moving forward, and continue to walk in faith to a new level of strength within that you never knew existed!

October 27

SAY IT WITH LOVE

When words are spoken from love, they soothe and heal. This is love in action, more powerful than any drug. But the same words spoken from fear or anger can tear flesh and cause wounds that can last entire lifetimes. The attitude behind your words determines if they will be a source of healing or hurting, so be mindful of how you say things. Speak to others the way you would want to be spoken to. Say it with love. Pause before you react with anger and scold someone by taking a step back. Remember the effects of your words and the motives behind them have power. Choose your words carefully, remembering that if you react with anger your words will be forgiven, but not forgotten. Say it with love, always.

October 28

KEEP THE FAITH

Don't let the darkness of the world blind you to the beauty that exists here on earth. Keep the faith. Unfortunately, life will be tough and sometimes we must endure situations that are unbearable. I know from my own experience of being raped that you can either let those experiences take you down or you can rise above them and not let suffering and darkness define you. I chose to live and rise above, making the best of my life in spite of this experience. During these times, turn to God, your source, to nurture your spirit and get you through. Over time, the darkness will fade as time heals our wounds and you will emerge with a newfound strength and courage. Our maker has created us to be resilient as long as we keep the faith.

October 29

Eyes Wide Open

Life's lessons come in many forms. We learn lessons through our mistakes as well as our successes. One mistake we all make is when new people enter our lives and we prejudge them based on physical appearance, their manner of speech, mannerisms, or other exterior manifestations. People I originally thought would be a nightmare became dear friends and conversely, others I put much stock into revealed themselves to be nothing but trouble with a selfish agenda. God puts people in our lives to teach us about ourselves. One of the biggest lessons I continue to learn is to be neutral when meeting others for the first time, keeping my eyes and mind wide open. To be a good judge of character I must be free of judgment. Have no preconceived opinion, but be kind, courteous, and polite. Let new acquaintances show me who they are before deciding. Let it unfold, keeping your eyes wide open.

October 30

PAIN TO GAIN

I have had to endure many setbacks and suffering in my life, but
I have emerged stronger with a newfound knowledge of myself.
This has helped me get through new obstacles that life continues
to bring. Sometimes, when I look back and see where I've come
from, it's astounding that I'm still alive after all I have been through.
I'm very grateful to God for saving me. One of the ways I thank
God is by sharing stories from my past—of how I overcame these
difficulties—with others. God uses these experiences as a true
testament of how my pain can become another person's gain in
helping and healing others. Sharing how I got through difficult times
in my life empowers both the listener and me, as we both witness the
possibility of not just surviving, but thriving. This sharing produces
a healing effect for both parties. Today, my life is an open book and I
welcome speaking to anyone who needs encouragement and healing.
Use your pain to help others gain.

October 31

HELLO, GORGEOUS

Too many people care how they look in the eyes of others. Why live in fear and bondage of what others think of you when you can be free—by taking off the mask you wear—and be authentic? Be yourself right now, whoever that is. Look in the mirror and say "Hello, Gorgeous." You are a unique creation, the only one in the world. God has created you with special talents, which can only be discovered by being your real gorgeous self. That is astounding! What a gift! Your true self is what the world is waiting for and our connection to that is where our happiness lies. Look inside and what do you see? Share what's on the inside and bring it out for the world to see. When we do this, we attract others who will join, support, and love us for what we truly are, not based on our fashion choices, the car we drive, or our newest electronic gadget. Live your truth and be free by God's standard, not the world's.

November 1

YOU CAN LET GO NOW

Are you constantly playing out scenarios in your mind until you
become obsessed? You can let go now. Try taking each problem you
struggle with and placing the outcome in the hands of God. Give it
all, one by one, over to your Creator to fix and let God lead you to
your rightful place. This is called letting go and letting God. Your
problems may be bigger than you are, and your fears about the
outcome may seem overwhelming, but they are not bigger than God.
We cannot see the big picture with our limited minds; only God can
and knows what's best for us. Let go. Let God control the outcome.
This is the simple solution, and it works when practiced. Soon you
will be at peace and know that wherever God leads you is where
you're needed. When you come to this place of acceptance you
will experience serenity like never before and the outcomes
will be far better than anything you could have thought of with
your limited mind.

November 2

GET OFF THE FENCE

Get off the fence and let your voice be heard. You'll never know if your input is what might change things for the better until you speak your mind. See both sides of a situation but have the courage to express your own conviction. Saying only what pleases others in order to look good or keep peace means sacrificing what you believe and over time, this insecurity will be your undoing. You cannot serve two masters and dual mindedness waters down your power. Standing up for what you believe does not always feel natural but over time will become easier. Courage is one of the superpowers God has given us and develops over time with practice, by thinking, acting, and speaking up each day as difficult situations arise. Own your power and become the person who is willing to come down off the fence.

November 3

LOSE YOURSELF TO FIND YOURSELF

Sometimes I spend too much time in my own head thinking about all my problems. Not a good place to be. This can be very debilitating, turning into depression. What alleviates this for me is performing simple acts of kindness. I lose myself in order to find myself and this releases happiness within me. I lose the part of me that is depressed by doing for others, no matter what I'm going through, and a new attitude emerges within me. These positive actions will snap you out of your rut and restore gratitude to your life. Works every time! But realize that to get results, at first it may be like walking up a muddy hill. Make a beginning anyway and keep going in spite of what you are feeling. Getting out of yourself is the simple spiritual solution to whatever ails you. My perspective changes from me, me, me to *what can I do for you?* When I place my life on a service plane for others, the blessings I give to others come back to me a thousand-fold. Place your problems on the back burner and help others today. Lose yourself to find yourself.

November 4

QUICKSAND OF NEGATIVITY

Fear is the enemy of happiness. In an instant, all it takes is one fearful thought to shift our thinking from happiness to dread, as we sink into the quicksand of negativity. We then ask ourselves, "How did I get here?" Recognizing the thoughts that trigger our fears and banishing them has become a way of life for me. By keeping vigilant each day and looking within, I become aware of what I am thinking about and can realign my thinking to positive thoughts, restoring my peace every time. I can turn my day around, many times if I have to, by using a simple daily exercise that helps me stay away from circling the quicksand. I ask myself questions, such as *Where am I? What am I thinking about? Why am I afraid?* This helps me identify the negative thoughts I harbor and turn them to positive thoughts. This daily spot-checking the inventory of my thinking saves me from unnecessary worry and keeps me out of the quicksand of negative thinking.

November 5

The Unspoken Words

Many times, it's not so much what you say—it's what you don't say. Conveying your feelings to others isn't always about speaking. I can make someone feel loved by the touch of my hand, comfort them by wrapping my arms around them, or by offering a wide smile. Love is an action, not a word. Love is communicated by the unspoken words you give by nodding your head or clapping your hands while watching a child perform in a play; the smile you give your partner when she performs an unselfish act to make others feel good about themselves; or cleaning up the kitchen after someone has prepared a delicious meal. There are so many ways we can speak without talking and make a positive impact on others. Love has so much power when our hearts are open and we speak love through our actions. This love touches and heals both the giver and receiver.

November 6

CHALLENGE YOUR FEARS

Fears that are not addressed grow bigger and bigger and can ultimately paralyze you, sending you into a full-blown panic attack. When we don't challenge our fears, we choose to let fear control us. When I got stuck in an elevator, I swore I would never ride in one again. This decision did so much harm to me and made my life difficult, having to walk the stairs everywhere I went. Then one day, I got a new job on the top floor of a high-rise building. I had no other choice but to take an elevator and in doing so, I began to challenge this fear, using prayer and asking God to help me. Slowly, the fear began to dissipate. Courage is the only remedy for any fear I have come up against in my life and is the by-product of walking in faith with God *through* the fear. Courage will emerge from within when you put God first and challenge your fears. Your palms may sweat and you may feel anxious, but those feelings will pass as you work through the fear and become fearless.

November 7

BUST A MOVE

Don't be afraid to act in a situation because you're afraid to make a mistake. You will never grow if every move has to be calculated and you believe it to be 100% correct before you proceed. When decisions have to be made, failing to act is a form of fear and will hold you back. Be brave and do what has to be done. You can always go back and fix it if you miss the mark. There are lessons to be learned in every experience and God wastes no opportunity, great or small, to teach us what we need to learn. So bust a move, don't stay stuck. Inaction will not move you forward. Even standing still, you are actually going backwards, feeding your fears. Coasting is an illusion. Complacency will be your undoing if you persist in your inaction. Bust a Move!

November 8

DIVINE INTELLIGENCE

Ever experience a "brain fart" and can't find the words you need?
Lose your stream of thinking? Your mind is so full it just goes blank?
Standing alone mumbling and stumbling trying desperately to
get your thoughts together, looking foolish? When this happens,
I quickly start praying. I unclog my brain and the logjam that I
am experiencing by using this simple prayer: *God, please let divine
intelligence flow through me now.* Saying it over and over will open up
the channel of divine intelligence that resides in us all and return you
to clear thinking. Soon, your mind will be at ease and all necessary
information will flow like water from a faucet. I use this prayer in
boardrooms when giving presentations, during exams at school,
speaking at meetings, or anywhere I am and in need of intelligence.
Just like God, it never fails.

November 9

DUMB IT DOWN

Here's some advice I was given that has proved very useful. You don't always have to have all the answers, and pretending you do doesn't make you smart. It's okay if you don't know. In fact, it's even okay to be dumb about something. Not one of us has all the answers. As a matter of fact, I am empowered when I don't know, because then I can learn something new. If you can wrap your mind around this way of thinking, you have begun to make small steps into a new life. Dumb and numb are good places to be because they are the prerequisite for learning. If you knew all the answers to everything, you would be perfect! And as we've learned together, perfection is a state of mind we can visit but never inhabit. Let yourself be dumb enough to learn new things. Next time you are asked a question and you just do not know the answer, try dumbing it down and respond with "I'm not sure. Let's find out." This will make you look smart.

November 10

GOD IS MY EMPLOYER

Have you ever thought about how you are being taken care of, how your needs are met? Money usually comes into our lives by paychecks from our current job. But who do we really work for? Who is our true employer? The employer we all really "work for" is God. Our current employer at the place we report for work each day is merely the channel through which God is providing for our needs, but God is the source. Never confuse the two. Knowing the difference is a blessing because if a job ends, I know God will open another channel to provide for my needs and I will be taken care of. What is my job description? My job description from God is to treat others the way I want to be treated. Give of myself with honesty, kindness, respect, and love. This is all God requires of me. When I adopt this attitude in all my affairs, I am living the way God wants and my true employer will always provide what I need.

November 11

THANK A VETERAN

God bless our military. They run directly into harm's way—not thinking about their lives, but our lives—courageously advancing toward the bad guys and becoming human shields for our safety. Some are hurt, seriously injured, and others make the ultimate sacrifice on our behalf to protect us and preserve the freedoms we enjoy every day. Have you ever thought about how brave and courageous these men and women are? They are at work all over the world right this second. These brave souls are putting their lives on the line every day, making enormous sacrifices for our great country. Their acts of bravery and unselfishness stir my emotions and bring tears to my eyes. Our nation owes them respect. When you see a veteran, thank them for their service. It's the absolute least we can do! They don't look for the attention but certainly deserve it. My dad is a veteran and I am so proud of him and all our military for their service. They are the true heroes of the world, risking their lives to make our world safer.

November 12

NIGHTTIME DRAMA

Do you suffer from nighttime drama? It's the phenomenon of tossing
and turning with what feels like a million thoughts swirling around
in your head, keeping you awake. Your mind is stuck in a loop and
it's driving you crazy. We all experience this at times and it can be
overwhelming. Nighttime drama is the result of taking daytime
drama to bed with you instead of letting it go before you sleep.
Holding onto resentments or fears, without discussion with another,
will wreak havoc with you when you try to sleep, thus causing
nighttime drama. Or, it can brought on by taking on too many
things at once. Everyone has their own triggers. Want to sleep
better? Try this: Every day, make it a habit to talk to someone
about your day, both the good and bad things that happened.
This will clear your conscience and ensure a good night's sleep.
When we properly deal with daytime drama, there is no more
nighttime drama. Pleasant dreams!

November 13

WORK ON YOURSELF

I can't fix you. No one can fix anyone else. Trying to fix others is like lighting a match next to a gasoline tank—sooner or later there will be an explosion. When someone is broken, they must find a source of strength within themselves in order to become whole again. We can help by leading others to faith, but everyone must do the work for themselves. We can hold someone's hand and be a cheerleader, letting them know how we got through tough times with God as our source, reminding them they are stronger than they know. But we cannot do their work. Once, I wanted the peace and serenity I saw in others, so I had to do what they did to get it. By their example and experience, which is the most powerful teaching there is, I too found strength I never knew existed. Later, I was able to become that example for others, but only because I worked on myself first.

November 14

GIVE A LITTLE, TAKE A LITTLE

A good negotiation always ends in a compromise. For a fair outcome for both parties, we must meet in the middle. A "winning at all costs" attitude may give you instant gratification but will never succeed in the long run and will most certainly lead to failure. If you want lasting success, you can't take advantage of others; that will only delay the success you crave and create bad karma you'll need to pay back in the future. It's always best to work for an equitable solution; do this by putting God first. Give a little, take a little is my strategy in life. In my business dealings, my personal relationships, and all my affairs, I always see God on both sides of the negotiation, which ensures that both emerge winners. A peaceful, fair solution will always work when you put God first.

November 15

TOLERANCE FOR OTHERS

What do you really know about the guy who just yelled at the checkout girl in the grocery store? Or the impatient driver on the road who is beeping at you to move faster? Truth is we don't know a thing other than their actions in that one moment. But then we judge and react. What if the guy who is yelling at the store is grieving the loss his wife? Or the impatient driver is on his way to the hospital to see his mother whose health just took a turn for the worse and he is worried he may not get to say goodbye? How would you react if you knew their stories? Our reactions or overreactions all begin with our perception. But we can train ourselves to question what we perceive. For me, this begins with preparation in the morning during prayer and meditation. I ask God to make me tolerant of others. To consider what unseen difficulties they may be dealing with. When we walk out of our house leading with tolerance, we can have a different view of events that unfold in our day and be a positive, healing force for good in the world. Being still and asking God to let you show tolerance to others is simple and something we can all practice daily to make the world a better place.

November 16

SHOW YOUR TEETH

There is much to be learned from the animal kingdom, especially from the common behaviors we share. Understanding how we're similar to animals can help us in our dealings with others. My dog, for example, shows her teeth as a way of telling me she has had enough. She is warning me to back up and stop doing whatever is it that's making her uncomfortable. She doesn't sit back and roll over! These are the signals she puts out to protect herself before she strikes if you don't heed her warning. It's a built-in defense mechanism God has given to both the animals and humans as well. Sometimes people will push us, and we need to let them know, in a courteous way, to back off. Of course, we shouldn't growl at them! But when others step over the line, find a polite way to push back and show your teeth. Let them know that under no circumstances will you roll over and play dead.

November 17

DON'T BLEND IN, STAND OUT

Don't follow what others are doing. Be original. Look within and use the strengths God has put there for you to bring out to the world. Each of us is created with different God-given talents, and part of our journey lies in discovering these gifts and using them to make a contribution to the world, whatever they are. Do what's in your heart and mind; don't worry about what others think of you. That's the way to find success. Imagine if all the great pioneers before us cared about what others thought? Bill Gates had an epiphany, and the most efficient computer operating system was born! He brought his ideas and ingenuity to the world and didn't worry whether or not it pleased anyone. Our ability to do many tasks on a computer would have never evolved without his vision. So many exciting inventions and discoveries would not exist if their creators had held their ideas in. So, don't blend in; expand and stand out, proud of what you are and the gifts you can offer to this world. We all have a part to play in God's plan. The world is awaiting your contribution to mankind.

November 18

911 Chicken

If you find yourself fighting with your partner over something trivial like how overcooked the chicken is and it erupts into a fight that makes you want to call 911 to settle your dispute, it's safe to say the relationship is as burnt as the chicken. Why do we let things get to this place? We continue on the path of "it will get better" or "I will change them," instead of seeing the truth of how things really are. Denial can be seductive. It speaks to us in ways that make sense at the moment but then always ends in disaster. We get into the relationship thinking we can change the parts of our partner we don't like and make them perfect or that a troubling situation will suddenly right itself. But we can never change anyone else, and poor relationships don't fix themselves. We must actively work on ourselves first to be the best we can be, then our relationship if we want it to succeed. Real love means we accept all parts of our partner, good and bad, or we can leave. You do have a choice. Staying and trying to change the other person always ends in 911 chicken.

November 19

WEAKNESS TO GREATNESS

You have the power to go from weakness to greatness by making the decision to change your mind. One day I woke up and said to myself, "I'm staying and not checking out." I no longer wanted to suffer or die from drug addiction and the onslaught of misery and pain it brought into my life. For the first time in my life, I reached for help and God turned my biggest weakness into the greatest experience of recovery and new life. Simple, but not easy, and attainable to anyone who has the will and wants to change. You do your part by complete surrender and abstinence and God does the rest by breaking down the walls of indifference and fear, using them as a platform to bring you from weakness to greatness. It's a choice I made and continue to make each day, choosing sobriety over a life of hell. Over time, my list of positive outcomes is growing as God continues to turn my other weaknesses into greatness by using this same principle on anything that is standing in the way of me living at peace.

November 20

WHEN ANXIETY COMES CALLING

Anxiety rears its ugly head from time to time, making our lives difficult. Resisting because we don't know what to do about it is scary and will only exacerbate the feeling. Don't fool yourself into thinking you can handle it alone; I never could. My desperation led me to seek professional help, where I learned that my anxiety is only a symptom of suppressed fears that need to be released. Keeping them inside is what caused my anxiety episodes. I was drowning in fear, guilt, and resentment. Through talk therapy, by openly and honestly sharing my worries, I was able to get to the root causes and release my demons. Over time, I gained a better understanding of myself and found the peace I desperately wanted. Today I have tools that help me to co-exist with anxiety. Now, when anxiety comes calling, *I* start calling. Calling out to others to talk about my problems, instead of burying them inside. I've learned that fear can destroy me if I let it, but prayer and meditation each day slow me down enough to stop my mind from racing, producing that calming effect I need.

November 21

THE RIVER

Did you know a river of knowledge flows through you that has all answers to anything you struggle with? We can wade into this stream of God consciousness through prayer and meditation and once you make contact, you gain a totally new perspective. Most people advocate that prayer changes things; but prayer doesn't change things, *it changes us.* Through prayer, my thoughts rise above my problems so God can show me the solution that I can never find with my finite mind. When we ask for help through prayer, we access this infinite mind and the floodgates open to unlimited knowledge we can never gain on our own. Tapping into this divine mind connects us to something greater than ourselves. The river will change us at our core. We gain insight and become enlightened to truth and wisdom, becoming reborn.

November 22

CHECK YOUR MOTIVES

Having a desire to "right the wrongs" is very different from "wanting to be right." These two states of mind are miles apart. One is done with love and the other with malice. But our minds can play tricks on us and camouflage a sinister motive underneath a worthy one, confusing the two. This is another way we allow our thinking to derail us and destroy relationships, jobs, and anything of value in our lives. Upon an honest examination of our thoughts, we can clearly see how we fool ourselves. Recommit yourself today and start checking your motives before you speak to or act toward others. This will save you a lot of unnecessary drama, salvage friendships, and keep peace in your soul.

November 23

GODPARENT

When I was asked to become a godparent, I had no idea what the role required. I found that in the Catholic religion, a godparent is entrusted with helping to raise the child in the church and foster their faith, and to serve as a symbolic parent if the child's parents should die. Those are weighty responsibilities, and it was an honor to be chosen. I have been blessed to be a godparent several times now and couldn't be any prouder of those children. They are a gift from God and a blessing in my life which I treasure. What God expects of me is simple: be a good role model who they can look up to and draw strength from. No matter what, always be there for them, giving them a shoulder to cry on; be the person they can rely on. I will always be in their corner. This fulfills not only what their parents want but what God wants too. Any adult, regardless of religion or the actual designation of godparent, can take on this supporting role in the life of a child they love, if the parents welcome the help. Raising children is so challenging in the modern world. Having another loving adult ready to assist is a blessing to both.

November 24

FOR THE FIRST TIME

Every so often I try this experiment. I pick something I am not happy with in my life and focus intently on just that one thing. It does not matter what, as long as it's something you are fed up with thinking or worrying about it. A job? A relationship? Whatever. Now, for one whole day, do this: THINK, SPEAK, and ACT only positively about the one thing you are unhappy with. See it brand new, as if for the first time in your life. Turn all the negative around and replace it with positive only, holding the highest thoughts you can muster for the entire day. When I practice this, I find my gratitude returns and new meaning emerges. My current landscape takes on a new perspective with more clarity to make decisions. The job you hoped to quit or the relationship you thought about leaving just might be the very thing you have wanted all along and almost threw away. Or, you may find it really *is* time to just let it go. Either way, you will be different *instead of indifferent* and intuitively know what to do.

November 25

THE LADDER OF GRATITUDE

Having a bad day? Can't remember how to return to your happy place? Well, I have a tried and tested solution. It's called the ladder of gratitude, and it will help you climb out of your problems. Whatever problems we face, gratitude will lift us up so that we can see the good in all things once again. It always does the trick by switching my mindset off the problem and into a solution. Sit down and make a list if necessary, of what you're grateful for, or just start remembering what is really important in your life, such as your health and the people you love dearly. These are the rungs that will carry you above your current situation to happiness once again. Whatever you are going through will fall away as you are brought back to a state of peace. I count my blessings and remember where I began and how far I have come and remind myself that things could always be worse. My perspective and faith are restored knowing I am never alone and God is always with me. Climb out of your unhappiness by using your ladder of gratitude.

November 26

HUMILITY OR HUMILIATION?

Never confuse humility with humiliation. There is a very fine line of distinction between the two and it takes some work to see the difference. Being contrite and admitting when you're wrong is humility at its best. When we clearly see our mistake, the harm done to others, and have a sincere desire to change our behavior and make our apologies, we experience humility. Leading with this attitude when making an apology, no matter what the response from others, will never leave you feeling humiliated. However, when we pay lip service to others by making hollow apologies just so we can get off the hook, and the apology is not accepted, we will experience humiliation. The difference is having an awareness of yourself and taking full responsibility for your actions, without blaming others. Being humble and having humility is a blessing that frees us from the bondage of self in every way and emancipates our spirit, keeping us closer to the goodness within us.

November 27

CLEAN UP YOUR ACT

I once heard that being messy was a sign of brilliance, so I ran with that—until my mess started affecting my life negatively. I was very unorganized and just threw things everywhere in the hopes that they would turn up sooner or later. I also used the excuse that it would take too much time to properly put things away. Little did I know than that this willy-nilly attitude was making my life hell. Being unorganized leads to a lot of problems we don't even consider until we start to examine our lives. You end up being late for everything since you don't know where you put your keys, phone, wallet, etc. Simply going to work or out with friends becomes an anxiety attack. Or, "Where is my new pair of pants? I just bought them." We rush around the house in a frenzy looking for misplaced objects while trying to beat the clock, causing ourselves stress when it's time to grab and go. Sound familiar? Without putting things in their proper place, this is what will happen. When this becomes a daily occurrence, it's time to clean up your act. Start by making a conscious effort to put things away and create a rightful place for everything. Becoming neat and tidy doesn't happen overnight, but with time and practice we get better and better. Also, you will find being organized actually saves time! How ironic! It's a good feeling knowing everything really does have its rightful place, including me, since I cleaned up my act.

November 28

YOU'RE GETTING WARMER

As a child, my siblings, friends, and I played a game. One person
hid something and all the others had to search for it. As we searched,
anytime we'd get closer to the object, the one who knew where it was
stashed, would say, "You're getting warmer." Conversely, if we moved
away from the object, we'd hear, "You're getting colder." To this day
the game continues since I am never done, still a work in progress,
still searching. When things seem to be falling into place and all the
parts of life are coming together into a beautiful picture, we're getting
warmer, moving closer to the life we've always wanted. If things are
not working out, usually this is an indication you're getting colder
and may need to move in another direction, perhaps rethink some
of the choices you made thus far. In life, we are always either getting
colder or warmer as we pursue happiness by the choices we make.

November 29

EXIT WITH LOVE

When I'm faced with having to detach from something toxic in my
life that will ultimately hurt me—whether it is a person, place, or
situation—I must always remember to move away with love and
respect for myself first, then for others. My actions upon exiting
anything in my life are going to follow me into the next chapter. If
I leave with good intentions, good will follow me and if I leave with
bad intentions, that will follow too. Always have an exit strategy
that brings good vibes and karma with you as you travel to your
next adventure or new beginning. By moving on with love
and respect, you are guaranteed to succeed and attract others
who are like-minded.

November 30

THE GREATEST LESSON

For me, trust must be earned, never given. This is one of the greatest lessons I have learned and continues to be important in my life today. We all want to give the benefit of the doubt and lead with our hearts, thinking people have good motives. While usually this is true, that's not always the case. I have made many mistakes giving trust where trust was not earned and unfortunately, I had to suffer. But through my mistakes, I learn. This doesn't stop me from believing the best of people, but now for my own protection, I am cautious and take the view that everyone's auditioning for a part in my life. I watch for their words to match their actions and vice versa. That is the verification I look for today in building trust with others. In the long run, taking time to develop trust will lead to relationships in which the most important thing in the foundation of all my relationships is trust.

December 1

SHOW ME YOUR FRIENDS

Do you know what kind of person you really are? Looking at yourself objectively takes time and practice and can make all the difference in becoming the person you want to be. Here is a very interesting exercise that helps me to better understand myself: Look around at all your relationships and people in your life, especially close friends. Now, ask yourself *what types of people are they?* What good qualities do you see in them? Also, what don't you like about them? (This is just as important for the experiment.) Once you determine this, take a good look. Who they are will reveal who *you* are. We always attract who we are, people who share our characteristics. My grandmother used to quote the ancient wisdom, "Show me your friends and I will show you who you are." This simple exercise will expose so much valuable information about you, far more than looking in the mirror. By studying the actions of others in your life, you will see yourself in them, good and not so good. This will help you determine what qualities you want to keep and what you need to work on to become a better person yourself.

December 2

THERE YOU ARE

How you enter a room full of people reveals a lot about yourself. Think about this: if you enter a room thinking, "Here I am, everyone," you lead with a selfish part of your nature, as if you are the center of the universe. Most times, no one notices you. But when you enter a room and your thinking is "There *you* are," you lead from the core of love and people will flock to you like bees to the sweet nectar of a flower. Everyone in the room will want to engage with you and will be attracted to the love and warmth you radiate. Our attitudes can make or break us, and we always have a choice of who we want to be in the world. Bring the love when entering anywhere and people there will respond with more love. New acquaintances will be impressed with your unselfishness and perhaps you will form lasting new friendships.

December 3

FEED YOUR SPIRIT

Solitude. Everyone craves it sometimes, and desperately needs it on occasion. In our busy lives, our minds get so scattered from the clutter we allow to accumulate. Some days we feel like taking our head off our body and sitting it on a chair. Give your mind a break by shutting off all thinking and planning and just be. Sit quietly and meditate, repeating, *Let divine order flow through me now.* These simple words allow you to slow down and feed your spirit, helping you remember who and what you are, emptying you of all cares and concerns. This simple, daily act of making time with your Creator will make all the difference in relieving the clutter and will put your life back in divine order and feed your spirit.

December 4

COLOR OUTSIDE THE LINES

Are you ready to color outside the lines and have some fun? Think about what would make you smile, then gather your homies, and make it happen. We work, work, work, and so we also need to play, play, play. Our lives can become so monotonous and we sometimes get cranky. Step out of your daily routine and do something you wouldn't ordinarily do. Fire up your imagination and color outside the lines today. Start planning it now. A new experience will refresh your spirit and create balance in your life. Sharing time and connecting with friends has become very important in my life. Whether it's just a few hours or longer, being with friends and loved ones breaks up the monotony of my life and puts the smile back on my face.

December 5

NEED NEW SHOES?

If you're unhappy and can't seem to get to a better place within yourself, think of others who are enduring far worse circumstances. Try on someone else's shoes. So many people are struggling—and some don't even *have* shoes! Take your pick. I assure you that if you think about how others' lives are in turmoil, you will see how good your life truly is. When you want to complain and run from your problems, remember there will always be someone worse off. Your perspective changes when you consider this, and you'll see your situation is not nearly as bad as you first thought. Turning my attitude around by mentally trying on others' shoes is one of the tools in my spiritual toolbox that brings me back to appreciating how good my life is today. So, step back into those size 9's you wear and be at peace.

December 6

NEVER INVINCIBLE, ALWAYS FLAWED

Many people in the world today think they are untouchable. They act as if they can defy the laws of the universe and somehow come out unscathed in situations where others would most certainly fail. As human beings, we will never be invincible and will always be flawed. No matter how much money, talent, or prestige you acquire in life, you don't walk on water; that is reserved for God and the masters. Only they are invincible. But many buy into this invincible mentality, stoked by the public's desire for heroes. The world puts people on pedestals, which only feeds the notion that they are Gods. This clouds their judgment and they begin to take foolish chances with their lives and the lives of others, which can cause harm. No one gets out of here alive. You are part of the same God as everyone else and when God calls you home, you are leaving. I write this cautionary tale as a reminder to us all before making decisions, based on a false sense of invincibility, decisions that may drastically affect ourselves and most importantly, others.

December 7

Start Auditioning

Some people only dream about finding a soulmate while others are busy attracting that special person into their lives. Which one are you? At first, I was convinced I'd never find Miss Right and of course I never did until I changed the way I thought about it. There is work to be done on our part; soulmates don't just arrive. I had to completely overhaul my thinking and change the way I looked at how to find her. First, I had to remove Miss Wrong to create a space for Miss Right. Next, I put down on paper all the qualities I wanted my soulmate to have and used it as a guide when dating. Then, I started "auditioning" prospects to find the right person who would fit my needs. Some of the qualities on that list were deal breakers, while others I was a little more lenient about and could compromise. But I took great care since this person was going to play an important part in my life. I kept the faith, never wavered or settled, knowing and believing the right one was out there for me. And then, my beautiful wife appeared. She has all the qualities I ever wanted in a partner and my life is now complete with her in it.

December 8

LOVE WITH DISCIPLINE

It's true that love has no boundaries but there are a few guidelines we must follow. We must be conscious of how we share love with others so it may be used to heal rather than hurt. Love without discipline can be harmful, just as discipline without love can hurt. Loving someone without employing a wholesome discipline in the relationship harms both parties; so does imposing discipline without love. After identifying this imbalance, the goal is righting it by loving with discipline. When we love with discipline, it gives us the support both parties need and creates a space for love to grow and flourish. Since our relationships with others are our laboratories for learning how to love, we must be conscious of how we express love. Love grows when it's properly tended, just like a beautiful plant or flower. Discipline with love is the perfect combination that will breed healthier and happier relationships.

December 9

THE GEOGRAPHIC CURE

In life, there is no geographic cure. Leaving the scene of the problem and moving to another house, city, or state is fruitless. What you need to realize is that you take yourself with you wherever you go. The problems you are currently running from will show up at the next destination, compounded, with only the names and faces changing. I've tried the geography cure many times in my life and it never worked. I also found you cannot wish or will problems away either. Pulling a Forrest Gump and running away from it all will never solve your problems, only make them worse. When life becomes too difficult and you want to run away, stay still and fight it out. Facing the problem, seeing your part in how things got the way they are, and accepting the situation is the only way to begin making plans to solve it and move forward. This attitude will bring you to a new place within yourself, not somewhere outside of yourself. It's there that you can turn things around. Real change begins within. Running only sells shoes, not solutions.

December 10

PULL BACK THE CURTAIN

When you pull back the curtain to your soul, what do you see? When my life was falling apart, I had to pull back the curtain and look very carefully to see who I was in order to fix what was wrong. The first step in changing begins with taking stock of yourself—an inventory of your strengths and weaknesses. This self-honesty helped me gain the necessary insight to help me change, and it's still part of my life today since I never stop growing and learning about myself. Seeing the truth about yourself is not easy but will set you free. It frees us from the lies we tell ourselves and come to believe, feeding our denial and keeping us in bondage. It's much the same as if you pull back the curtain in your home, allowing the light to shine in, helping you see things more clearly. The light is symbolic of truth, which helps and heals any situation. When I live in truth, I live close to God since truth is another aspect of God. I begin to know my value as a human being, having dignity for myself and being comfortable with who I am.

December 11

SOMETIMES THE ANSWER IS "NO"

There are times I cannot do something for others, so sometimes my answer to their request is no. No doesn't mean we don't care about others; it means we are taking care of ourselves, which is perfectly acceptable and healthy. Self-care is not about abandoning or hurting others, it is affirming our needs first. We can't be there for others if we don't care for ourselves first and so in some situations, the loving response is "No." If saying yes means putting my life in turmoil to please others, that creates a no-win scenario for both parties. Saying yes to please others will end up making me resentful and blaming others for a situation I have created. Both people get hurt when it could have been different had I merely said the word "No." Saying no when you need to is a tool for self-care. No is a small word but when we use it properly, it restores my mental health.

December 12

DISCUSSIONS WITH MY POSITIVE SELF

Each day I have discussions with myself. Most times they are
productive. I ask the important questions and listen for answers
with a positive outlook. Some answers make complete sense, others
nonsense. I use deductive reasoning, common sense, and positive
thinking as I delve into my brain for the solutions and decisions
that have to be made that day. I then say a prayer asking God for
direction, so I can tap into the great intelligence of the universe.
Keeping positive thoughts produces positive actions, which will then
produce positive experiences. This is my key to success. Our thoughts
are powerful. Depending on which ones we choose to include in
our conversations with ourselves will decide success or failure.
Keep the discussions with yourself positive or you will be
consulting with an idiot.

December 13

JOURNEY OF FAITH

There are many paths to faith. Pick one and take a few steps every day diligently until you succeed in finding what you need to get by in this life. It's not important how fast you get there, but how you travel. Finding your faith is a very private journey. Some of us experience a call to faith when pain comes and life becomes too big for us to live anymore. I found my long-lost faith at the bottom of a bottle of alcohol. Whatever the circumstances, remember that God can go by any name you choose. No one has a monopoly on faith; you get to pick the religion or spiritual practice that makes sense to you. There are so many fine paths that will get you to a God you can love. God is omnipresent and omniscient and wherever you are, God is. It doesn't take much to contact this power, just prayer and a willingness to be found. God is standing by awaiting your call and will meet you on your terms, wherever you are in your life. Reaching out is the first step. Then, you take one small step, followed by another, and you will be on your own journey of faith.

December 14

THE WALLS

In the past, I never opened my heart to others for fear of rejection. The walls I created within me, walls I thought were protecting me, actually kept the love I craved away from me. I read somewhere that I had to start taking chances and express love into the world if I wanted love in return from others. By trying this, I found that when I let the love within me show up, it attracts the love inside others. We link up like a good internet connection. Breaking down the wall and putting the vibes of love out for others attracts the best from them, and you both become blessed. Now, when I step out in love, love follows me and others feed off it with miraculous effect. This love heals, protects, and nurtures us. Try it and you'll find a new dimension of living that, until now, was untapped and will bring a far better life than anything you were living. Break down your walls and start sharing love.

December 15

THE GRACE OF GOD

Grace is such a lovely word. Grace's power is awesome. When the word falls off my lips, I begin to melt into the beauty and calmness of my Creator. Just by saying this precious word aloud, my soul is illumined and I'm hopeful once again that I can break free from all the bondage of this world and be forgiven for my trespasses. We all need grace when we fall. Grace is the vehicle God uses to lift us up and make us new once again. I have experienced God's loving, saving grace many times. Grace has held me up and restored my dignity when I thought all was lost and I was hopeless. If your heart is open and you are truly ready to heal and begin again, grace will come to you. With grace, you can move your life into another direction, which you can never do under your own power. This healing, miraculous force of grace is what we all need at some point in our lives. I thank God every day for grace.

December 16

IT DOESN'T COST A THING

Here is something we can all do to bring happiness to ourselves and others, something easy that doesn't cost a thing: offer a simple compliment and be kind to all who cross your path today. After all, who wouldn't like to hear a nice compliment? To the stranger on the elevator, tell them they look nice in that color. Most times a simple compliment will surprise people, and perhaps delight them and turn their day around. The smile that may spread on their faces will acknowledge how much they appreciate your gesture. We never know what others are going through in their lives, and a simple nod of kindness shown to others just might be what they need to change their mood. At work, ask how a co-worker's family is doing and really listen intently, showing true concern. These simple acts set the stage for many blessings to come in your life. By spreading good will to all you meet and greeting others with a smile, we brighten and enlighten the world with selfless giving of our time and of ourselves. There is no greater gift we could give to ourselves, others, and the world and it doesn't cost a thing.

December 17

MY SOUL MATE

The thing about romantic love is that you never know when it might arrive. You hope and pray for your soulmate to show up, but life just continues. Then one day, God sends that special someone masquerading as a co-worker, a neighbor, a stranger on a train, or a friend of a friend. Before you know it, you are instantly smitten and feel things you never felt before. A great force inside is pulling you two together and you cannot do anything to stop it; the magnet is too powerful and the attraction is overwhelming. This is how it happened for me. Suddenly, I realized she was the one I wanted to spend the rest of my life with. I asked, made myself ready for her, and God delivered to me the love of my life, the person who will be beside me for the rest of my days. We love and support each other, will always have each other's back, and no matter how many times we may argue, I know she will never leave the room. Having her in my life, and the special bond we share, is a gift from God. To me, this is what it means to find your soulmate.

December 18

KNOCK, KNOCK

What will you do when temptation comes knocking at your door? Who will you choose to be? The choices we make each moment decide our future. So, what's it going to be? When you hear that knock, will you step up or fall down? We must be ready for temptation by being awake and vigilant in identifying our weaknesses. Over time, staring down temptation will lead us to become the best version of ourselves. This takes a lot of work and honesty and is only achieved one day at a time, like water wearing away the rough edges on a stone. Life is full of temptation and we need God's strength to help us overcome. By surrounding myself with others who are like-minded in the face of temptation, I receive the power necessary. There is strength in numbers; we are powerless alone, but together can ignore even the strongest, most insistent knock.

December 19

SERENITY THROUGH PRAYER

Many people scoff at the idea of prayer. They say it's for the weak. Well, I've found they are right! When my life fell apart, I was at my weakest and ran out of answers. That was the moment when I began to pray. I didn't know what I was praying to; I just started talking out loud hoping someone or something was listening. A friend suggested I try the following popular prayer:

Serenity Prayer

God, grant me the serenity to accept the things I cannot change,
the courage to change the things I can,
and the wisdom to know the difference.

Reinhold Niebuhr (1892–1971)
American theologian

At first it felt very unnatural and awkward but over time a sense of peace and calm came over me. The words to that prayer are very healing and connect me with a serenity deep within. Now I start each day with a set of prayers, or sometimes I just speak to God from my heart. Prayer helps me get centered in peace and gives me a better perspective to start the day, raising my heart and mind above the daily frustrations, and connecting me to the calm within.

December 20

NO STUPID QUESTIONS

Willful lives produce many difficult lessons. By doing whatever we want without stopping to weigh the consequences or consider how our actions will affect others, we burden ourselves with more problems. Why do we do it? Speaking for myself, my own willfulness was because I never wanted to be told what to do by anyone. I thought I would look stupid for asking questions, so I plunged ahead, asking no questions at all. But there comes a time when we must listen to others to avoid the many pitfalls of life, or we dig deeper holes we might not be able to climb out of, getting buried altogether. When I had the realization that my supposed "best thinking" had brought me to a point where I needed drug and alcohol rehab, I began to ask others to help me. I began asking questions, asking for direction with my thinking process and decisions that I needed to make in my life. I asked how others handled difficult situations. I asked so many questions, wanting to learn from their experiences. I was finally willing to listen to others and found the only stupid question is the one you don't ask.

December 21

WAKE-UP CALL

Sometimes people we care about need a wake-up call. You might be the one who has to deliver it. If someone you love needs to be told the truth, not some watered-down version of it, then get ready and dial. When you have their attention, hit them right between the eyes with the truth; this is the very thing they need to awake them from their slumber. I have been on the receiving end of many such wake-up calls and have also had to deliver a few. The wake-up call can be a loving response a friend may need from us to shake them up at their core and become responsible for their actions or inactions and see clearly once again. It helps them put their lives back in order and on the path to peace once again. Give them the truth, with love, and pray they hear it. Many have blessed me by loving me enough to tell me a truth that has changed my life and I will do the same for others. I no longer avoid the conversation, nor will I tell you what you want to hear. I will love you enough to tell you the truth with all the love I can possibly summon. Who knows, that wake-up call you make may save someone's life. The wake-up call you get might save *your* life.

December 22

APOLOGIES HELP US

Apologies given to others are the gateway to freedom and peace
of mind for the person who does the apologizing. They lead to
forgiveness, which we all need. It took me some time to realize that
an apology is not only for the recipient, but for me as well. Apologies
are like bridges to your own soul that connect you to your source
of love and freedom within. An apology clears our side of the street
and makes things right between you and the other person, but also
between you and your God. By waiting for others to apologize
first you are only rationalizing your own behavior and not taking
responsibility for your part. But when we take responsibility for our
actions, this paves the way for true forgiveness of our spirit and helps
us move on and grow spiritually. Apologize to others for the harms
you have done or whatever was done to you—don't wait or delay.
Do it for yourself.

December 23

THE BENJAMINS

My ideas about money needed an overhaul. In my childhood home, I grew up hearing, "Money is the root of all evil." Hence, my takeaway was that having money was not a good thing and remaining poor would keep me humble and closer to God. This mindset kept success away from me, because I repelled money and remained poor. It was later in my life when I learned the actual wording in the Bible is, *For the love of money is the root of all evil.* Hearing this made me question myself and my beliefs and led me to think about money differently. Earning money and having money are good things when we work honestly and with integrity. Cheating others, stealing, and ill-gotten gains stemming from a love of money are what makes it the root of all evil. The importance we place on acquiring and keeping money and the methods we use to get it make all the difference. If I am hurting others in order to make money or to hoard it for myself, then I might have more money, but I will have kept God out of my life. It is only by working honestly and saving and spending wisely that I can keep God in my life. When money is no longer the focal point of my life, the Benjamins can accumulate for good. It's become very simple for me now—money is an exchange of energy. What's important is the energy I put into earning with integrity and sharing with compassion.

December 24

INSPIRE OTHERS

Our biggest failures can open the door to our greatest success stories. When you turn your unsuccessful life around with hard work and determination, you can influence and motivate others. Do that. Inspire others today. Tell them how you made your big change, step by step, honestly. We all need encouragement that feeds the soul. It's necessary for others to witness the miracles we have been blessed with to serve as a model to help them gain strength and courage on their own journeys. Inspiration based on shared experience helps others know they are not alone and they too can overcome their difficulties. Many people have inspired me throughout my life by their example, filling me with hope, empowering me, and spurring my own desire to change. In turn, I give back by showing my gratitude and sharing my experience, strength, and hope with others. Show some love today to someone who is lost and needs direction. Be an inspiration.

December 25

KING OF KINGS

Today is special to me. Merry Christmas to all my brothers and sisters who celebrate! I love remembering the true meaning of this day. He came here with a plan of eternal salvation and healing for all who believed in Him and followed Him. He was my brother and your brother who God sent to show us by His example that there is no death, only everlasting life in God's kingdom. He was ridiculed and humiliated for His beliefs but never wavered, standing firm with God, delivering messages of hope, love, healing, and strength. Through His suffering, His selfless acts restored faith for many, giving Him the much-deserved title, King of Kings. He has inspired people and nations over the centuries with His powerful acts of mercy and miracles and continues to do so today. My deep appreciation, admiration, faith, and love grow every day for Him as I walk with Him, my savior Jesus Christ.

December 26

GIVE IT AWAY

The surefire way to get whatever you need in any situation is to give away the very thing you seek. I never knew I had the power to manifest my needs simply by giving away what is lacking. If I want love from others, I must be loving. If I want peace from a situation, I must be peaceful. If I want to be forgiven, then I must forgive others. What I extend is what I eventually will bring into my life. I once had a very troubling relationship and all we did was fight, like two children always wanting to be right. Then one day, I realized if we were to ever get to a place of love, we had to stop hurting each other. Self-examination revealed I was not giving love; therefore, I was not getting love. That's when this idea exploded in my head and I became willing to try a different approach. I began giving love to this person, slowly, and our relationship transformed into one of the best in my life. The change was dramatic and taught me that, sometimes behaving contrary to the negative way you're feeling or thinking can achieve a positive result. Doing the same old, same old, will bring the same results unless we give what we want.

December 27

COME CLEAN

What are you afraid of? What fear are you holding onto that is wreaking havoc within you? Is there something in your past you work hard to conceal? You have a choice. Keep these secrets and become sicker or share them with another and get better. Whatever it is that is troubling you, there will always be someone who has a similar issue, someone with personal experience who can help. Finding that person who can identify with what you are going through is a blessing and nothing to be ashamed of or embarrassed by. We all think our secrets are the worst things anyone has ever done and we will have to carry them to the grave. My secrets almost put me *in* the grave. But when I came clean with another person, I no longer had to succumb to the guilt and remorse I was holding onto for many years and found ways to move forward and heal. I also realized I was not alone. My secrets were not so unique. Come clean and share your burdens with another and let your healing begin.

December 28

MOLLIE BLUE, I LOVE YOU

Mollie Blue is her name. She is the most precious dog who has healed my heart on so many levels, bringing unconditional love always. Mollie never has a bad day. Her life here on earth is simple—to love and please others. She does both so very well. With her by my side, I always feel loved, appreciated, and most of all, grateful we rescued her. But really who rescued who? She may not have survived the terrible start she had in this life if it weren't for the loving people who put their lives on hold to rescue innocent animals. The beautiful women who rescued my Mollie, Jane Wallace Hynum and Christine Conte, are some of God's angels here on earth, and I am very grateful to them for their selfless acts of love they perform for all animals. They are my heroes and God holds a special place for them as I do. The world is a better place with them in it and my life is forever changed because of them.

December 29

GIVE IT TIME

Many things in life need time to develop. Whether it's a new book you are writing, a new relationship, project, habit, or situation—we must let things unfold naturally and organically. Giving these things their due time will save you in the long run. You will have given yourself the opportunity to slowly watch and observe as life works itself out to a natural, happy ending, and you adapt to the newness. Settling into our new lives must be taken slowly to allow ourselves to absorb the changes. Perhaps this change is a rite of passage that requires adjustments and a new outlook. Pushing and rushing can lead to disaster on all levels. I have ruined many opportunities in my life by pushing forward, when being cautious would have been the better approach. Try to give time, time.

December 30

SUCCUMB OR OVERCOME?

When you begin a new venture, remember that fear may pay you a visit, trying to tell you that you are not good enough, or that no one will be interested in what you have to offer, that you shouldn't bother wasting your time and money on something that will fail anyway. This is fear trying to sabotage you, and we must overcome, not succumb. We have a choice. There are many forces in the universe. Fear is a powerful one; we can succumb to it if we are not vigilant in our faith. Fear waits and will rear its ugly head whenever we try to better ourselves. Expect it to show up and be prepared. We can rise above fear through our faith and learn how not to let it rule our lives. Once we acknowledge fear, it loses its power over us and falls away. When fear creeps in, call its bluff. Don't succumb. Overcome.

December 31

LET IT ALL FALL APART

It's the eve of a new year. A time when most of us reflect on the past year and think about what we want to change in our lives. Perhaps there's a festering situation or problem, and you've had enough. Go ahead and let it all fall apart. Let it go and start anew. If you are circling the drain, you might get swallowed up if you don't make a move right now. Surrender to what is and start off the new year with a new you. If you find you are no longer in control and you are wasting your time, knocking your head against the wall trying to save something that is hurting and destroying you—just stop and let it all fall apart. Your resistance is the only thing holding you back. Another life is awaiting you that will be far better and can only begin by letting go of what is now. Sometimes in life things need to fall apart in order to fall into place. Let it. Let go. From this action, God will guide you to a new foundation to build your life on and it will be a blessing.

About the Author

LUANN SMITH

Luann Smith has overcome many obstacles in her life, emerging from it all with a newfound strength and awareness of herself. She shares her life experiences openly and honestly, spreading hope to all who struggle and as a way of thanking the universe for saving her life from her addictions. Luann lives with her wife Betty Ann, daughter Max, and their dog and cat, Mollie and Jax. She enjoys getting together with family and friends and is an excellent cook who can throw down with the best of them. Luann can be contacted at info@luannsmith.com.